To the Fourth Generation
(of computers)

THE ULTIMATE FRONTIER

As man becomes machine, he becomes increasingly the participant in his own evolution. Some of the results seem incredible. Yet some of the results are already a matter of scientific record!

- Machines *more* intelligent than man
- Medical marvels like radio pills to monitor bodily functions . . . the atomic pacemaker . . . a steam engine *inside* the body . . . artificial blood, veins, skin, and skeletons of stainless steel
- Computers coupled to the brain for objective psychoanalysis
- The new man who can kill or stop a car with a flick of an eye . . . relive experiences he never had . . . feed on nothing but solar energy . . . grow gills to live underwater

This is our brave new world. It holds far more promise than peril. It will not begin on some distant tomorrow—it has already begun!

Books by David M. Rorvik

As Man Becomes Machine
In His Image

Published by POCKET BOOKS

AS MAN BECOMES MACHINE

THE EVOLUTION OF THE CYBORG

DAVID RORVIK

PUBLISHED BY POCKET BOOKS NEW YORK

Grateful acknowledgment is made for the use of the following copyrighted material: Excerpt from the article "Development of a Brain Prosthesis" by L. R. Pinneo taken from *Primates in Biomedical Research*, edited by G. H. Bourne, Academic Press, Inc., 1972. Reprinted by permission of the publisher. Excerpt from the article "Visual Prosthesis by Electrical Stimulation of Primary Visual Pathways" by L. R. Pinneo taken from the book *Visual Prosthesis: An Inter Disciplinary Dialogue*, edited by T. Sterling, et al. Copyright © 1971 by T. Sterling, et al. Reprinted by permission of Academic Press, Inc. "The Wave of the Future" by David M. Rorvik. First appeared in *Look* magazine. "Someone to Watch Over You (for Less Than 2¢ a Day)," by David M. Rorvik. First appeared in *Esquire* magazine. Copyright © 1969 by Esquire, Inc. Reprinted by permission. "Electronic Nirvana" by Dr. Daniel E. Noble from *Proceedings of the IRE*, The 50th Anniversary Edition, May 1962. Reprinted by permission of the author and The Institute of Electrical and Electronics Engineers, Inc. "And It Will Serve Us Right" by Isaac Asimov reprinted from *Psychology Today Magazine*, April 1969. Copyright © Communications/Research/Machines, Inc. Reprinted by permission of the copyright holder. "Slaves or Masters?" by David M. Rorvik. Originally appeared in *Playboy* magazine. Copyright © 1969 by HMH Publishing Co., Inc. From the book *Brave New Baby* by David Rorvik. Published by Doubleday & Company, Inc. "Emotions and Malignance" by Howard B. Miller. First appeared in July 1970 issue of *Science Digest*. Copyright © 1970 by The Hearst Corp. Reprinted by permission of *Science Digest*. Pinneo, L. R., Erickson, E. E., and Kinney, R. A. "Selective Deep Brain Stimulation with External Electrodes." In D. Reynolds and A. Sjoberg, ed., *Neuroelectric Research*, Chas. C. Thomas, Springfield, Ill., 1971, 405–425. "Fifty Years of Teaching Machine" by Dr. Harold A. Zahl III, *Proceedings of the IRE*, May 1962. Reprinted by permission of the author and The Institute of Electrical and Electronics Engineers, Inc.

POCKET BOOKS, a Simon & Schuster division of GULF & WESTERN CORPORATION
1230 Avenue of the Americas, New York, N.Y. 10020

ACKNOWLEDGMENTS

Grateful acknowledgment is hereby made to *Esquire*, *Playboy* and *Look* for permission to reprint portions of my articles which they first published. I would also like to thank the many doctors, scientists, engineers and technicians who gave so generously of their time and patience in helping me prepare this book.

CONTENTS

INTRODUCTION

THE MELDING
OF MAN AND MACHINE

Tralfamadorians, of course, say that every creature and plant in the Universe is a machine. It amuses them that so many Earthlings are offended by the idea of being machines.

—Kurt Vonnegut

The human body is the magazine of inventions, the patent office, where are the models from which every hint was taken. All the tools and engines on earth are only extensions of its limbs and senses.

—R. W. Emerson, 1870

I live on Earth at present, and I don't know what I am. I know that I am not a category. I am not a thing—a noun. I seem to be a verb, an evolutionary process—an integral function of the universe.

—R. Buckminster Fuller

Apart from its alliterative appeal, the word "meld" is powerfully descriptive of what is beginning to take place between man and the more seductive of his machines. Forged, one suspects, by a *Time* magazine writer, the word "meld" is the felicitous marriage of "melt" and "weld," the first a force of destruction, the second a force of construction. But, far from ripping itself asunder on the opposing rocks of its foundations, the word coheres beautifully, implying, by sheer force of its sound, a perfect, intimate blending of objects— even, or perhaps *particularly,* of things as seemingly inimical as the forces that make up the word itself. Of such things as soft, sensuous and intensely mortal flesh and hard, cold and relatively immortal calculating machines.

First comes the melting, a destruction, yes, but not an absolute destruction, not an end in itself, but rather a submission, an accommodation, an act, in this context, almost of love. A giving so that something can be gained: man abandoning part of his old identity, melting so that he can be forged anew, fashioned in such a way that he can be welded to machines that amplify his senses, extend his grasp, deepen his understanding of himself and his world. *Together,* man and machine become something more than either could ever have been alone, an entirely new order of life, an evolutionary chimera, a cybernetic organism, a cyborg.

But is this the way it will really be? Will the man-machine interface always hum with electrical fidelity, with each neurone and integrated circuit seeing eye to eye, firing off in perfect sequence? Or will the sex life of man-and-machine develop some unhealthy kinks and incompatibilities? Will one partner demand more, the other give less? Then what? Will the stronger break the embrace and strike out alone, ultimately to establish an unyielding hegemony over the other? What if there's never any melding on man's part at all, just melting while intelligent machines of the sort discussed in the first chapter of this book achieve self-sufficiency and finally the upper hand, opting not to merge with man but merely to tolerate him and finally to dominate and possibly even eliminate him, if need be?

But then surely the notion that artificial intelligence can surpass that of man, that computers can evolve to a state of consciousness and attain a will and a way of their own, totally free of man's influence, belongs in the realm of science fiction novels. Or in films like *2001: A Space Odyssey,* in which Hal, a thinking, talking, hearing, lip-reading computer, comes close to taking over command of a spaceship, and in *The Forbin Project,* in which another computer, designed for defense purposes, takes over the world after making a compact with a similar Soviet computer. It would, perhaps, be comforting to believe that all of this is nothing more than the stuff of the imagination, something that can never be realized in fact. Such wishful thinking, however, is readily dispelled by a number of cybernetic experts who have already designed, as we shall see, robots able to do man's work with enviable speed, precision and efficiency, computers able to read, speak, see, learn and even feel. Some of these machines have even acquired personalities of sorts, complete with sexual identities, hates, fears, loves, hopes and dreams.

But a computer or a robot more intelligent than man and able to reproduce itself and ultimately create machines more intelligent than *itself?* Could such a thing ever come to be? Yes, it is "a real possibility," says Dr. N. S. Sutherland, professor of experimental psychology at the University of Sussex and a leading computer expert. Nor is Dr. Sutherland alone in this startling conviction. Many of his colleagues here in the United States agree. Some even go as far as the imaginative Dr. Isaac Asimov in asserting that it will not only be possible for computers to "take over" but that it will be all to the good when they do! In light of man's performance on the planet to date, Dr. Asimov's argument, discussed in detail in Chapter One, "Man-Machine Rivalry—Will Intelligent Machines Replace Mankind?" may be difficult to refute.

Still, one has every right to hope that man and machine can, as both progress through time and space, establish an *entente cordiale* based on a mutually beneficial relationship. It is on that optimistic note that most, but not all, of this book proceeds, on the best, rather than the worst, of what is possible. This is not to deny that the worst, from man's point of view, could happen and that many of the "advances" of the biocybernetic sciences could, like so much else that has passed for "progress," constitute just so many more nails in our collective coffin.

After some of the fearful pronouncements of Chapter One, we turn to "Channels of Peaceful Coexistence—Emergence of the Medical Cyborg." This creature, the medical cyborg, is evolving in our midst at a prodigious rate of speed. He comes in a variety of sizes and shapes and forms, equipped with such diverse appurtenances as dacron arteries, ceramic hip joints, steel bones, silicon breasts, pacemakers, electronic bladders, plastic corneas, artificial intestines, lifelike mechanical hands and arms, cutaneous sighting systems and on and on. Under development are even more ambitious "spare parts," including plastic hearts, artificial lungs, implantable mechanical kidneys, synthetic glands, rubber bone joints, plastic skin, even artificial cells. At the same time man is gradually coming to rely upon a still more complex artificial "organ," the computer, to diagnose his ills and stands at the brink of an era in which his brain and body will be linked directly to these machines for guidance and treatment of both mental and physical ailments.

Eventually, it has been hypothesized, it may be possible for man to "trade in" *all* of his bodily parts for more durable, if not in fact immortal, mechanical counterparts. Even those with sturdy natural organs may opt to trade them in at some point in the ultimate program of "preventive medicine." A man whose family history is annotated with heart disease may, for example, want to buy a plastic heart, once they are perfected, rather than risk middle age with a vulnerable flesh-and-blood pump. Similarly, a woman may voluntarily forsake her natural facial skin for the imitation stuff even before her own starts to sag, so that no one will ever notice the difference. Others with failing sex glands may be able to purchase youthful potency over the counter at a medical spare-parts consortium—then have the apparatus implanted by their own doctors. Amputees, before too long, may be able to purchase a variety of bodily extensions that can be plugged into joint sockets, or removed at will, rather in the way that one can insert a variety of useful tools into the same power unit, depending upon the task at hand. Such enviable versatility might even lead to "planned amputations."

The concept of "total prosthesis," the exchange of all bodily parts (except the brain) for more reliable mechanical ones, recalls a statement made once by Thomas Edison: "The body is just something to carry the brain around in." The body, in other words, is not the man—the brain is. In this light, total prosthesis seems somehow less shocking, more practical. Still, man thus modified will no longer really be man. He will be a cybernetic organism and, contrary to what many might think, almost certainly capable of greater feeling than ever before; as a cybernetic entity he will be able to alter his sensory inputs and outputs with new versatility. He might, for example, easily communicate with his fellow cyborgs via microwaves and even such complicated sensory inputs as an orgasm might be triggered by something as simple as a particular type of electrical pulse, telemetered to his brain via implanted electrodes. Eventually, some are convinced, man will discard even his brain, having first programmed all of its knowledge and personality into the computer part of his being.

If such should ever occur, man would be transformed into something virtually immortal. The medical cyborg, even as presently constituted, raises new questions about death and aging. Already heart-lung machines and the like keep people "alive" long after that point at which they would, only a few years ago, have been declared dead. *What* is death? and *When* is death? are questions that will become increasingly difficult to resolve as artificial organs and mechanical life-support systems become widely available. Ultimately, owing to this new technology, we may have to face such questions as: when should death be *imposed* on the individual? If one can go on trading in failing parts indefinitely, the death rate will dwindle away to nothing, resulting in an intolerable population explosion. Fortunately, scientists are beginning to propose guidelines to cope with some of these problems, indicating in the course of their warnings their confidence that science, for better or worse, *will* be able to build even the complicated cybernetic systems necessary to maintain the disembodied brain.

Indeed, in animal experiments, brains, completely removed from their natural environment within the body, have already been artificially sustained in the laboratory. It is only a matter of time before the brain, some would say the "mind," of man is similarly isolated and then "implanted" in a mechanical "body." Such an organism (or even one in which the brain is "drained" into a computer and then discarded) would represent the ultimate melding of man and machine, constituting a victory for both entities: man-mechanized, machine-humanized. Together, man and machine can achieve things that neither can alone, both becoming something more than they were as single organizations of matter, peacefully coexisting in an evolutionary symbiosis.

Still other channels of peaceful coexistence are explored in Chapter Three, "Reaching for the Stars—The New Era of Participant Evolution." Here, a whole new class of man-machine systems, designed to help man hurtle through space and other hostile environments, to extend his senses and amplify his strengths, are examined in detail. These include a dazzling array of hardware now under production, most of them with appropriately exotic names, such as "cybernetic anthropomorphous machine systems (CAMS)," "powered exoskeletons," "teleoperators," "androids on remote manipulators," "master slaves," "telefactors," "brain-computer symbiotes," and so on.

These are systems that, in the words of one of their developers, allow the man in the cybernetic loop to "pick up and examine samples of the lunar surface while remaining on earth; repair an underwater pipeline from a surface ship; manipulate radioactive nuclear fuel elements in a hot cell; lift a ton-sized load." Some also permit man to kill whatever he happens to be looking at with the mere flick of an eye or, with the same minute exertion, bring an automobile to a grinding halt. Less ominously, they also allow doctors to diagnose and even treat a patient's ills while miles away from that patient. In all of these systems man serves as brain and central nervous system. The machine provides the muscle and the reach and amplifies whatever signals it receives from its human nervous system. Most of the machines are "slaved" to man with "feedback" and "spatial correspondence" concepts that will be enlarged upon later, so that the two components of the cyborg operate in harmony with very little or no conscious control on the part of either.

It is in this chapter that we come to terms with the new concept of "participant evolution," the notion that man can assume some of the controls that were previously the exclusive province of Mother Nature and thus change himself along whatever line he desires. No longer can man be said to be entirely the offspring of nature, the creature of natural selection. Science is providing him with the technology to become his *own* maker. Dr. Edward L. Tatum, Nobel Prize winner, calls man's growing ability to engineer his own genetic future "the most astounding prospect so far suggested by science." And Cal Tech biologist Robert L. Sinsheimer terms it "one of the most important concepts to arise in the history of mankind," adding that, "for the first time in all time, a living creature understands its origins and can undertake to design its own future."

Participant evolution proceeds along two fronts: the genetic and the cybernetic. On both fronts man is, with ever increasing momentum, entering into his own evolution. The genetic or biological "revolution," as it has been termed, is founded primarily on the discovery of the structure and operation of DNA and RNA, the nucleic acids that constitute the very essences of biological inner space, containing as they do the chemical code of life and the blueprints by which all living structures are designed. That discovery and subsequent findings permit man to begin manipulating his genetic molecules in an effort to become master of his own heredity.

"Genetic surgery" is the term Dr. Tatum and others have applied to describe manipulation of DNA and RNA. Dr. Tatum foresees the day when geneticists will be able to delete undesirable genes, insert others and mechanically or chemically transform still others, foreordaining, at the molecular level, the physical, mental and even racial characteristics of the incipient individual. All of this, says Dr. Joshua Lederberg, another Nobel Prize-winning geneticist, could become a reality within one or two decades.

Stunning as this prospect is, even the gene tinkerers and the genetic engineers, limited as they are to the world of flesh and blood, may have to take a back seat to the medical engineers and biocyberneticists who are beginning to broaden further the concept of participant evolution by joining man with machine to extend, amplify and accentuate his strengths in ways that even the most extensive "genetic surgery" could never accomplish. The cybernetic approach, moreover, is more flexible than the genetic. Rather than breed special individuals for particular space environments

19

through genetic engineering, for example, why not *temporarily* alter the individual cybernetically (in ways that will be detailed in Chapter Two) so that, once the mission is over, he can function normally in the accustomed environment? Genetic participation in evolution, in other words, tends to be permanent; the cybernetic approach can easily incorporate versatility and *reversibility*.

The man amplifiers permit us to enter into intimate unions with machines, providing us with abilities to operate with a minimum of fuss in what would otherwise be hostile environments. A space cyborg one week, an underwater cyborg the next. But a man *genetically* engineered to breathe through gills is going to have a difficult time adjusting to outer space or, for that matter, coming back up on dry land.

Still, it is wrong to establish a genes/machines dichotomy. The true cyborg is a combination of the two, and in some cases genetic engineering might be necessary before man can be satisfactorily wed to machine. It might be used, for example, to encourage the body to accept readily the implantation of foreign materials, of electronic circuitry, artificial organs and the like. It might also be used to alter bodily proportions so that the body can better accommodate mechanical additions. It has even been suggested that the genetic material might be manipulated in such a way that the body would create cells capable of performing like the memory circuits of computers, making in effect a literal, living machine!

Envisioned in Chapter Three—this time by the scientist who coined the word "cyborg"—is a world "peopled" by nothing but copulating computer entities, men in new organizational packages. Here, too, is a vision even more utopian: mind encoded in electromagnetic energy, completely disembodied, free not only of flesh and blood but even of integrated circuits.

Even without such wonders, or horrors, depending on how you feel about abdicating the flesh, the cyborg revolution crackles with surprises, many of them either completed or in the making right now. General Electric, among others, has a whole laboratory full of them, all undeniably useful, one or two a little frightening. There's "Hardiman," which will enable you to lift 1500 pounds with one hand; there's a Walking Truck that will turn you into a four-legged mastodon able to flick railroad ties out of your path as though they were mere toothpicks; there's a two-legged pedipulator in the works that could lengthen your stride by several yards; there's also a "minipulator" contemplated that would serve as a "slave double" on reconnaissance and sabotage missions (if it gets caught it will self-destruct, blowing up not only itself but also its captor; the human operator, acting as brain and nervous system, meanwhile will be left high and dry at some remote site).

Then there's ARMS—a cyborg system that will let you reach and feel and even work across 22,000 miles of space without ever leaving earth. ARMS—this, too, a GE project—is designed to repair orbiting satellites and spacecraft and to help rescue astronauts in distress. It is more than an orbiting robot, for without a man in the loop, experiencing everything the machine (or android, as it is called in this case) experiences, it cannot function properly. Just why it is so much better than a preprogrammed automaton or robot will be explained in Chapter Two.

A similar but more sophisticated system that will be examined in the same chapter is the "telefactor" system. Telefactors could push man's senses into deep space—to the moon and even beyond—while leaving his body safely on earth. More exciting yet, telefactoring provides a means of letting hundreds, even thousands, of individuals share the thrills of space travel or underwater exploration without subjecting them to any of the risks. It makes possible, in short, the sort of "feely" TV envisioned so often in science fiction. It also promises to have an impressive number of highly practical applications in education, sports and medicine.

In Chapter Four, "Mechanizing the Mind—Brave New World of ESB," we enter the sometimes ominous realm of electronic stimulation of the brain, better known simply as ESB. Not to be confused with ESP or extrasensory perception, ESB embraces a number of new procedures, "including electroanalgesia," "electroanesthesia," "electrosleep," "electroprosthesis" and some others that might, for lack of more descriptive terminology, be called "electrosex," "electromemory" and "electroeuphoria."

Electronic stimulation of the brain is just that—direct electrical stimulation of carefully selected cerebral sites via stainless steel electrodes surgically implanted in the brain. Proper stimulation can evoke all sorts of emotional and physical responses; it can turn raging lions (of the human variety as well as the feline) into gentle lambs and gentle lambs into raging lions. It can obliterate even the most disabling pain without the aid of any drugs, lull you into sleep, fill you with pleasure that surpasses sexual orgasm and bring back childhood experiences with such vividness that you cannot distinguish between the real and the hallucinatory.

ESB can also be used to "record" activity occurring deep within the brain, again via implanted hairlike electrodes. With ESB, neurophysiologists are finding it possible, for the first time, to provide detailed "maps" of the brain, linking specific brain structures with specific cognitive, emotional and physiological events and functions. In many ways these deep probes into the still mysterious mind may prove to be of much greater significance for mankind than probes into those other great frontiers: outer space and the ocean depths.

For the physically handicapped, ESB could mean the difference between a dull and useless life and a full and relatively active one. Already under development, and showing a great deal of promise, are "electroprosthetic" devices that help stroke-paralyzed individuals move again. Experiments with animals indicate that implanted electrodes can be used to stimulate parts of the brain not affected by the stroke with such precision that the previously immobilized animals not only move again but do so in a coordinated and almost natural fashion. With computerized controls (and no

encumbering equipment whatever) the victim has only
to punch a few buttons in order to instruct his brain
—electronically—as to where, when and how fast he
wants to move. Research is also under way in other
ESB prostheses, including some that seek to restore
sight to the blind and hearing to the deaf.

ESB, bound to have sweeping impact in all of the
medical sciences, may prove a particular boon to the
psychiatric profession. Indeed, it has already been used
to control rage in individuals prone to outbursts of
violence. (It has also been demonstrated effective in
curbing other seizures, such as those associated with
epilepsy.) And it appears that ESB far surpasses
hypnosis in "regressing" patients to early childhood.
The "experiential hallucinations" that it can evoke,
when properly used, can supply psychiatrists with a
wealth of information about their patients, information
that might take years to dredge up from the subcon-
scious using conventional therapy and analysis. Even the
emotionally well person may want to relive some past
(particularly pleasurable) part of his life, and, in fact,
it has been suggested that the elderly might eventually
be able to pass the time away by reliving parts of their
youth after plugging into an appropriately programmed
ESB machine.

Indeed, for a few cents in electricity, *anybody,*
properly wired with electrodes, might be able one day
to plug into a computer console at home, dial in the
number that corresponds to a particular experience and
then lean back and enjoy. It is conceivable, some experts say, that by firing off electrodes in the right
sequences, under computerized control, a person might
be able to experience just about anything that man can
imagine—a climb up Mount Everest, an evening alone
with a beautiful young lady or a rugged male (sex and
other bodily features tailor-made by the computer to
suit individual taste), a trip to the moon. If these
pleasure machines ever become economically feasible,
one thing will be certain: television and the movies
will be in serious trouble.

Man could be in trouble, too, if ESB technology

were to fall into the wrong hands. An electrical engineer named Curtiss R. Schafer provides us with just a hint of the nightmare that could ensue if totalitarians or fanatical efficiency experts in high places should one day decide to "optimize" society by robotizing it. Such individuals, Schafer suggested, might decide to implant electrodes in the brains of babies shortly after their births and then dictate their every action via computer-modulated radio control. If this sounds wildly farfetched consider the fact that animals have already been successfully robotized in just this fashion. Summing up some of these experiments, Dr. José M. R. Delgado of Yale University, one of the foremost practitioners of ESB research, notes that laboratory animals have been made "to perform a variety of responses with predictable reliability, as if they were electronic toys under human control."

Here again we must return to the notion of participant evolution—something that has a nice, democratic ring about it—and concede that only a *few* might be doing the participating. Such was the case in Aldous Huxley's prophetic novel *Brave New World,* in which genetic engineering is used to establish a biochemical hierarchy in which some are decidedly more equal than others. ESB, similarly, could be used to establish an electrohierarchy, with a powerful "Electroligarchy" governing the masses with the aid of computer-controlled electrodes. A frightening future of this sort is envisioned in Chapter Four, in which, in place of Huxley's biochemical strata, there are electronic castes. At the bottom are the "Neutrons," individuals with the greatest number of implanted electrodes, robotized for low-grade labor. Above them are the "Positrons," with fewer electrodes, designed for white-collar work. And above them the "Electrons," the most creative members of society with fewer still electrodes (but with enough to insure their loyalty to the ruling zero-electrode Electroligarchy).

But, you are thinking, even though the technology for such a world may be at hand, we will never permit such a thing to happen; without the cooperation of the

24

masses no oligarchy, no matter how powerful, could ever implant electrodes in the brains of every one of its subjects—or even of a majority of its subjects. This is probably true, but why be so confident that the all-important ingredient in the scenario, cooperation, will not be forthcoming? The "doomsday denigrators," as a columnist in *New Scientist* calls them, too often overlook man's willingness, in fact his eagerness, to "cash in" on the latest wonders of Science. To many people, Science—with a capital S—is the new god, to be followed, obeyed, idolized as something that can do no evil, that can solve all ills. But the masses submit to the implantation of electrodes, even if the powers-that-be lure them in by promising "electronic nirvana?" Nonsense!

Or is it? As the aforesaid columnist in *New Scientist,* Donald Gould, points out: ". . . these doom-denigrators believe they are being no more than sane, sober, and sensible when they dismiss the likelihood of Man using the new instrumentalities of science in obscene or disastrous ways. They are (by some trick of intellect) apparently able to forget Hiroshima and Nagasaki and Belsen. They are—these doom-denigrators—apparently unable to accept the idea that not all the 3500 million human animals with whom they share this world also share the Scottish Presbyterian ethic.

"And that," he continues, "is why the doom-denigrators should study the story of the schoolchildren of Omaha, Nebraska, some 5000 or 6000 of whom have, for two years or more, been taking a brain stimulant called Ritalin. This mass, communal doping has been undertaken on the advice of a local specialist in child health, and with the approval and help of teachers and parents and because of a hunch (no more) that it might improve performance in the classroom."

Before word of this "experiment" leaked out and responsible scientists began to point out the considerable dangers of such indiscriminate "treatment," the parents of Omaha no doubt felt that they were giving their consent in the best interests of their children; many, no doubt, experienced smug satisfaction with the program, fully expecting that their Ritalin-doped little darlings would, before long, begin showing up their stimulant-starved counterparts in Chicago, New York and San Francisco. That an experimental drug, taken over a long period of time by growing children, could have unpleasant or even disastrous side effects in months or years to come seemed to be of little or no concern to anyone. The tiniest possibility of providing something artificially that Nature overlooked—in this case brains—is demonstrated to be sufficient, in the Omaha case, to make everyone throw caution to the winds.

What will occur then when ESB—the effects of which *can* be highly desirable and, unlike Ritalin, have been so demonstrated—becomes widely available? It seems logical to assume that people will not only be willing to let medical technicians wire their brains with electrodes but that they will even *pay* to have this done.

Optimism is, for the most part, restored in the final chapter of the book, "Liberating the Spirit: Toward 'Electronic Yoga' with BFT." BFT stands for biofeedback training, and it labels yet another sort of man-machine symbiosis, this one designed to put mind over matter and thus liberate the body in ways never before possible. Again, BFT represents a prime example of peaceful coexistence between man and machine, surpassing in harmony even the man with the plastic heart and the dacron arteries. BFT uses electroencephalogram (EEG) machines and other monitoring devices to find out what is happening inside the brain and the body and feedback displays (such as sounds, lights, colors, graphs) to *tell* the individual what is happening.

Sounds simple—and basically it is. But the therapeutic effects of BFT can border on the incredible. It has been compared with both the LSD experience and the meditative tradition. Some call it "electronic yoga," others "electronic nirvana." It puts you in touch with inner space just like LSD but, unlike acid, leaves you in full control of your senses. And, unlike Zen and other types of meditation, it doesn't take years of practice to master. It gives strong indication of being safe and predictable and promises to revolutionize psychology and medicine as nothing else ever has.

Bio-feedback pioneers say that BFT could, among other things, completely replace many drugs, help people overcome anxiety, overwhelm numerous psychosomatic ills, facilitate learning, enhance memory, alleviate heart and circulatory diseases, illuminate many processes of the mind and even provide access to previously unimagined experiences, thus not only defining the dimensions of inner man but also extending those dimensions in the process.

BFT is already attracting a cultish following across the country and there is some danger that it could be abused just as some of the hallucinogenic drugs were. Its benefits are potentially so great, however, that many scientists warn that we must not be frightened away by the misuse some might put it to. The dangers are certainly not as great as those associated with certain drugs or with ESB, and, in fact, some researchers believe that BFT can be used to strengthen an individual's resistance to propaganda, brainwashing and even the subtleties of everyday advertising.

BFT units designed for use in the home are already under experimental production. Hence it may not be long (within five years, according to many scientists, much sooner than that according to others) before you can hook yourself up to an inexpensive BFT machine and begin learning how to control your brain waves, body temperature, heart rate, respiration, blood pressure, intestinal acidity and many of the other things said for years to be beyond conscious control. You might use it, as some already have, to quell or even dispel migraine headaches, to ward off feelings of anxiety, to curb appetite, to reduce the desire to smoke, to achieve a feeling of serenity or even euphoria without any sort of chemical stimulant, to attain an optimum state of mind for study or memorization, to relax muscle spasms and so on. These are but some of the more conservative uses to which BFT can be applied; its proponents (who recently formed their own scientific society) envision much, much more as we shall see.

Man has always regarded his machines, though things of his own making, with something akin to awe. Man is constantly, in his legends and his lore and now, too, in his laboratories, attributing to them anthropomorphic features. And, as often as not, we have regarded machines as possessing the power not only of man but of superman; hence the evolution of robotical fantasies from the time of the ancient Greeks to the present, when fantasy begins to impinge on reality. The Greeks had a phrase that is still with us today: *theos ek mēchanēs,* better known in the Latin as *deus ex machina.* It means, literally, *a god from a machine* and today denotes an entity, be it god, man or simply thing, that emerges suddenly and unexpectedly to provide a seemingly miraculous solution to a seemingly insoluble conundrum or difficulty.

Deus ex machina promises to remain part of the language, since seemingly insoluble problems are more than ever with us. But it will almost certainly assume new significance as the god, or, as some would have it, the "ghost," in the machine turns out to be the man himself, albeit man of an entirely new order.

ONE

MAN-MACHINE RIVALRY

WILL INTELLIGENT MACHINES REPLACE MANKIND?

In someone's words, the human being is the only computer produced by amateurs.

—Dr. G. L. Haller
of General Electric Company

Do not be bullied by authoritative pronouncements about what machines will never do. Such statements are based on pride, not fact.

—Dr. Marvin Minsky
of the Massachusetts Institute
of Technology

I hope we have solved the integration problems between human races before we face the problems of integration with robots.

—Dr. J. P. Eckert
of UNIVAC

A favorite subject of magazine cartoonists these days is the computer as mental defective. Several years ago, in fact, the computer had already become the butt of so many jokes that a writer was commissioned to investigate the phenomenon for the now defunct *Fact* magazine. The writer (John Dempsey, now a cultural critic for the Boston press) found that the average man, far from expecting a god or a benevolent ghost to spring from the mammoth computers that are increasingly governing our affairs, fears instead that these machines will eventually take his job away from him, thus replacing him as a producer and a provider, possibly even as a father and a lover. He fears, in short, that the computer is about to unman him.

If the computer's maddening efficiency and speed have one refrain it's that old singsong: anything you can do, I can do better. And so when the computer does make a boo-boo (very rarely indeed, when you examine the amount of data each one handles during its average workday, which can be twenty-four hours long) everyone rejoices! And soon a few minor errors (actually, more often than not, the fault of the computer's human programmers) are compounded into a major liability, so far as the computer's reputation is concerned. But the computer, impervious to petty emotions, goes on performing day after day with ever greater versatility and virtuosity. And so poor man continually has to step up his disdain, look harder for errors, guffaw a little louder each time he finds one. A sad state of affairs, but an understandable (read *human*) one.

Still, man no longer feels that he can afford to live without the computer. It is everywhere: in his offices making out the pay checks; in his schools calculating IQs and grade-point averages; in his food-packing plants, directing the addition of chemical additives; in his factories, coordinating the complexities of assembly lines; in his better automobiles, regulating fuel injection; in his "think tanks," working out the subtleties of scenarios for World War III; in his space vehicles, meting out, with infinite care, the components of a life-giving atmosphere; in his effluent society, keeping tabs on pollution; in his hospitals, analyzing a patient's ills; in his banks and credit agencies, keeping track of who owes whom what and when; in his department stores and mail-order houses, processing sales; in his giant airplanes, doing more than a "man-sized" portion of the work. Nearly everywhere and still breaking into new fields, new jobs, even creating some new ones of its own.

Already a white-collar worker and, in many instances, back-shop manager, the computer as a minority entity is making a phenomenal ascent. Before long it may occupy what amounts to high executive slots in many commercial undertakings. Ultimately (and here even the courageous begin to get nervous) it may take over some of the "front desk" jobs of the meet-the-public genre. Fine for other computers, but how will man hold up? Better than ever, say *some* computer enthusiasts, pointing out that well-trained computers are less likely to commit costly *faux pas* than are nervous front-desk receptionists of the human variety. Properly programmed computer-receptionists will lend a scrupulously deaf ear to flattery, bribery and general cajolery, admitting to the inner sanctum over which they stand guard none but the "worthy." Similarly, a computer instructed to lie under certain circumstances ("I'm sorry, Mrs. Smith, but your husband is tied up in a conference right now") can be counted on to do so with a perfectly "straight face."

Finally, the computer can be expected to invade, in great number, that last sanctuary of man, his home, his castle. At first the computer and the computerized robot can be expected to make a modest entry, serving as humble doorman, guard, cook, bottle washer, chambermaid, grounds keeper. Then, however, the mass-produced domestic computer will begin playing games with the "master"—*literally*. Computerized card partners and chess opponents are already in the works. It would be "uppity," to say the least, to win all the time—particularly so soon after discarding the apron, dustcloth and dishtowel.

Eventually the clever computer will go from mere playing to more serious business—like managing the household budget and finances, providing menus for the entire month with an unemotional eye on each individual's waistline, politely but firmly reminding various members of the family of their social and civic commitments, of their dental and medical appointments, teaching Junior how to read or master the *new* new math, providing Dad with tips on the stock market (probably requiring a somewhat more expensive computer than most will be able to afford) and Mom with tips on the optimum color combinations, hair styles, make-up and so on for any particular occasion or mood.

Before long, it appears, the computer will figuratively be sitting at the head of the table, and man, though in a sense unmanned, will probably like it. After he gets used to it, that is, which shouldn't take long, with the computer activating automatic equipment to mow the lawn and water the garden. Better anyway than a nagging wife. When it comes to the big decisions, like whether to buy a new car, how much better it might be to give the computer the responsibility. Then, if something should go wrong, and if money spent on one item should suddenly be needed for another, the wife won't be able to say, "I told you so." Or, if she does, she'll have to say it to the computer. What a joy for the henpecked husband when the computer curtly comes back with something like: "Your comments are unacceptable in present form."

"SOME OF MY BEST FRIENDS ARE ROBOTS"

Where will it all end? With robots in control and man in the zoo? Or will man heed that well-weathered bit of advice—if you can't beat them, join them—and *become* the computer? Is there really much need for alarm now, or even for interest and concern? Or is artificial intelligence just another illusory star in some far-out scientist's blue sky? Let's look.

A physicist addressing a gathering of automaton enthusiasts in Europe several years ago declared that "some of my best friends are robots," and then, without so much as a smile, promised, "I'll even let my daughter marry one—just as soon as you fellows come up with a model than can speak well enough to say 'I do' at the appropriate moment, see well enough to put the ring on the right finger, emote well enough to kiss her properly and work hard enough to support her in the manner to which she has become accustomed."

The physicist, obviously, was confident that he was not about to lose a flesh-and-blood daughter or, worse yet from his standpoint, gain a stainless steel son. Today, he would have to be considerably more cautious about making such a promise. He might have been in trouble even as early as October 1967, when Bruce Lacey, a British actor and inventor, designed a robot that served as best man at his wedding. The robot handed over the ring at the right moment, threw confetti and even kissed the bride, actress Jill Bruce, with foam-rubber lips.

In a more serious vein, factories across the country are already using robots that work sixteen hours a day without complaint and with only occasional "illness," robots capable of supporting entire families since many of them "earn" as much as $20,000 per year each. There are about two hundred of these blue-collar automata in the United States today and, though they are all blind, deaf mutes of decidedly limited intelligence, they already have clocked at least 500,000 hours of nearly flawless work in jobs that, for humans, at least, are either dangerous or unspeakably dreary.

And outside the factories—in university laboratories across the land—a generation of robots is rapidly evolving, a breed that can see, read, talk, learn and even feel. At the Weizmann Institute of Science in Israel robots have been developed that embody man-like muscles. At the University of Texas computer programs are being developed for the purpose of eventually providing robots with sexual identities, personalities, hates, fears, loves and hopes. At Stanford intelligent machines with hands and eyes are being constructed that can see well enough to move around obstacles, plan ahead rationally and carry out missions that have been only partially outlined by human controllers. At Mullard Research Laboratories in England other machines are being taught to read so well that some scientists believe robots will even be capable of comprehending bad handwriting. Are there any limits?

Dr. Marvin Minsky, professor of electrical engineering at the Massachusetts Institute of Technology and a pioneer in the field of artificial intelligence, recalls that "our pious skeptics told us that machines would never sense things. Now that the machines can see complex shapes, our skeptics tell us that they can never *know* that they sense things." But, he cautions, "do not be bullied by authoritative pronouncements about what machines will never do. Such statements are based on pride, not fact. There has emerged no hint, in any scientific theory of machines, of limitations not shared by man. The rate of evolution of machines is millions of times faster, because we can combine separate improvements directly, where nature depends upon fortuitous events of recombination." With the realization of genetic engineering, of course, man can step in and take over some of nature's "recombinations," but Dr. Minsky's point is still well taken: it is far easier to manipulate machines than it is to manipulate man.

Similarly optimistic about the future of robots, N. S. Sutherland, professor of experimental psychology at the University of Sussex and a computer expert, states flatly that "there is a real possibility that we may one day be able to design a machine that is more intelligent than ourselves." Dr. Sutherland has made a comparative study of the basic components of the human brain and the robot brain (a digital computer) and finds the latter in several respects the more promising.

"There are all sorts of biological limitations on our own intellectual capacity," he says, "ranging from the limited number of computing elements we have available in our craniums to the limited span of human life and the slow rate at which incoming data can be accepted." Dr. Sutherland sees no such limitations in store for the computers of the future. No one is certain how many bits of permanently retrievable information the conscious portion of the mind can accommodate in a lifetime, but many scientists think one billion is a reasonable estimate. Existing computers can transfer that amount of data from one magnetic memory to another in a scant twenty minutes.

Thus, Dr. Sutherland points out, "it will be much easier for computers to bootstrap themselves on the experience of previous computers than it is for man to benefit from the knowledge acquired by his predecessors. Moreover, if we can design a machine more intelligent than ourselves, then, *a fortiori*, that machine will be able to design one more intelligent than itself."

THE MONSTER MYTH DISPELLED

Dreams of the perfect robot, one capable of surpassing man's most brilliant feats without succumbing to any of his erratic weaknesses, have occupied philosophers and scientists since the time of Homer. It was that poet, still read and reread for his mastery in probing the mythic desires of man's collective unconsciousness, who perhaps first envisioned automata: the mechanical golden girls who were at the beck and call of the smith god Hephaestus in the *Iliad*. The girls caught the attention of such scientific visionaries as Roger Bacon and Rabbi Low, and by the eighteenth and nineteenth centuries mechanical men and women were the life of avant-grade parties from Berlin to Boston.

George Moore created a gas-powered mechanical man who could walk along at a brisk pace while smoking a cigar, and Gaston Deschamps titillated his audiences with a mechanical snake charmer of the female sex. Perhaps the most fondly remembered of the early robots, however, was Wolfgang von Kempelen's chess player, a dark-visaged automaton garbed in the flowing robes of a Turk. He took on all comers, defeating each of them, including the Emperor Napoleon. It took the detective talents of Edgar Allan Poe to reveal the secret: a midget chess expert tucked under the robes.

It was in 1818 that Mary Wollstonecraft Shelley's classic horror novel *Frankenstein* was published, an event that was to have more than a passing impact on the way in which society would regard robots and other man-made men for decades to come. Mrs. Shelley (the second wife of the poet) was inspired by the scientific work of the Italian anatomist Luigi Galvani, who demonstrated that dead muscles could be persuaded to contract by exposing them to electrical current. The discovery galvanized society, suggesting as it did that electricity was one of the essential secrets of life and that, moreover, man could use it to restore or even to create life in the laboratory.

Mary Shelley sensed the ghoulish potential of all this, artfully exploiting it in her novel about an enterprising anatomy student named Frankenstein who assembles a human collage of assorted dead parts and then enlivens his creation, an eight-foot monster, with an electric charge. The monster, miserable because he is doomed by his unpretty parts to a bleak social life, turns on mankind, outraged at the species for interfering with Mother Nature. Moral indignation is expressed in the form of multiple murder (with Frankenstein himself succumbing to a relatively gentle death by remorse) before, at last, the monster recedes into the polar regions, which, in case you haven't been keeping up, now house an impressive bevy of spent monster-things, including "The Blob."

From *Frankenstein* on, society tended to regard man-made creatures as inherently evil, bound to turn on their creators or, at the very least, cause them endless pains in the neck. Karel Capek almost certainly had Frankenstein's monster somewhere in his mind when he injected the word "robot" into the public consciousness in 1920, via his now-famous play *R.U.R.* (Rossum's Universal Robots). *Robota* is the Czech word for "worker," and in the play robots are created by man to take care of most of the heavy labor; instead, true to the ghost of Frankenstein's monster, they turn on their creators. The pattern was set. Science fiction writers from that year on portrayed robots in the R.U.R. mold: malignant, unnatural creatures who inevitably try to destroy mankind. Implicit in this hidebound characterization is the notion that man, in creating artificial life, oversteps the boundaries allowed mortals and therefore must be punished for his *hubris*, the sort of overweening pride in his own abilities that has always, in literature, got him in trouble with the gods.

About the only science fiction writer (as he modestly acknowledges) with sufficient imagination to portray robots as benign, or at least indifferent, beings is Isaac Asimov. In more than a score of short stories and novels he has characterized robots as machines "created by human beings to fulfill human purposes." He rejects the idea that the creation of robots places man in God-forbidden territory and insists instead that automata, like other mechanical devices, are simply the product of man's engineering ingenuity. In place of mysticism Dr. Asimov posits science—the applied science of "robotics," a term he coined and now in general use to describe the study, design and manufacture of robots.

That he was able to march to the beat of a different drum, instead of participating in "this wearisome parade of clanking monsters, forever parodying Shelley and Capek," Dr. Asimov declares, is attributable to the fact that he got on well with his father. People fear robots (and computers) for the same reason that fathers often fear their sons: because they are afraid that the sons might prove mightier than the father. Dr. Asimov cites the case of Zeus and his brother Poseidon who compete enthusiastically for Thetis, a comely sea nymph—only to lose all interest when the fates advise them that Thetis will give birth to a son more powerful than his father.

Writing in *Psychology Today* (April 1969), Dr. Asimov explains how he came to make robots respectable: "When I began to write robot stories in 1939, I was 19 years old. I did not feel the fright in the son-father relationship. Perhaps through the accident of the particular relationship of my father and myself, I was given no hint, ever, that there might be jealousy on the part of the other or danger on the part of the son. My father labored, in part, so that I might learn; and I learned, in part, so that my father might be gratified. The symbiosis was complete and beneficial, and I naturally saw a similar symbiosis in the relationship of man and robot."

It was on the basis of this philosophy that he projected in 1942 his now famous "Three Laws of Robotics," which are often quoted today by the manufacturers of industrial robots, apparently in an effort to quell the fears of those humans who must work alongside them on the assembly line. They are:

1. A robot may not injure a human being or, through inaction, allow a human being to come to harm.

2. A robot must obey the orders given it by human beings except where such orders would conflict with the First Law.

3. A robot must protect its own existence as long as such protection does not conflict with either the First or the Second Law.

Today, Dr. Asimov notes, most science fiction writers adhere to the three laws, although of late, he concedes, there has been a resurgence of robotical monsters, notably Hal, the creation of Dr. Asimov's friendly

39

rival, Arthur C. Clarke. Hal, the thinking-talking-seeing and all-knowing computer featured in the film (and the novel) *2001: A Space Odyssey,* turns on his human cohorts during a long space journey and kills most of them by cutting off their life-support systems. "This disturbed me, and impressed me as a retrogressive step," Dr. Asimov complains, "but it doesn't seem to bother Arthur at all." In an interview with Clarke, shortly after the release of the monumentally successful film, he told me that he considers Hal anything but a monster. Instead, he regards him as the actual and intended hero of the film. "When you read the novel, there's no question," he says, "but that Hal's the good guy. He's just been mucked up by his human programmers."

Dr. Asimov's sentiments are really not very much different from those of Clarke. Clarke makes it clear that he is on the side of the machines, and Dr. Asimov, while appearing to be protective of man, is really being protective of robots. He insists that they are not mindless monsters banally bent on the destruction of mankind. Yet he stops far short of saying they will not ultimately replace mankind. And there is nothing contradictory in his outlook; replacing something for good reason is clearly different from harming it just as a matter of course. But before we consider the whys and wherefores of a computer/robot takeover, let's examine the state of the art.

THE SAGA OF CLYDE THE CLAW

Although the very existence of the term "robotics" seems to suggest a definitive science, there is still considerable confusion about just what constitutes a robot. Science fiction (of the non-Asimovian mold) has persuaded many people that a robot is a cast-iron dummy who walks like a hopeless arthritic and talks like Tonto. One wonders, naturally, just how manlike a machine has to be in order to qualify as a robot. Is a robot really very much different from a computer? What distinguishes a robot from ordinary automated equipment? Are remote-controlled machines robots?

First of all, a machine needn't look anything like a man to qualify as a robot. Its manlike or anthropomorphous nature must manifest itself in performance, not in appearance. As for computers, when thinking in terms of robotics, it is best to regard them as the brains of the robot—single, although very vital, organs in the encompassing whole. Remote-controlled machines belong in a class apart from robots whenever their operation depends not on built-in programs or artificial intelligence but on intimate mechanical or electronic links with their human "doubles."

In general, what sets robots apart from most automated equipment and imbues them with their manlike nature is a flexible memory and a more dynamic feedback mechanism. In ordinary automatic manufacture, a machine can, for the duration of its life, perform only one task with one specific product or material. A robot, on the other hand, is like a man in that it can be trained (programmed) to do a great number of tasks. It can paint cars one week, load conveyor belts the second and pour cognac the third. Old memories are easily erased and new knowledge just as easily inserted.

Feedback, present only in primitive form in most automated devices, permits the robot to monitor its own actions and correct its own errors. It is the same trait that tells man how hard to push against a door in order to open it or how much leverage to apply in order to lift a box off the ground. A widely adjustable sort of feedback, then, helps free robots from the lockstep controls of ordinary automated equipment, the feedback of which is as static as its task, without permitting them to metamorphose into clumsy monsters crushing or flinging away everything they touch. Feedback has as many channels as there are senses, though not all of these channels have yet been incorporated into robots. As far as I know, anyway, there is not yet a robot that comes equipped with olfactory feedback, i.e., the sense of smell. But there no doubt will be before long.

Whatever the incredible promise of robots in the future, it is the hard-working and intriguing, even if not particularly glamorous, industrial robot who defines the current state of the art. Without his clearly demonstrated success in the working world, his more exotic brothers (and sisters) might not be in the laboratory right now.

It was George C. Devol, an engineering genius, who became the Roger Bacon, the Rabbi Low and the Wolfgang von Kempelen of the twentieth century. But unlike his imaginative predecessors, Devol had at his disposal the technology necessary to realize his dreams. Devol, in the early 1950s, was disturbed by two ugly realities of the industrial world: the prevalence of dreary, dehumanizing "put-and-take" jobs in factories and plants and the disastrous obsolescence rate of automated equipment. Devol realized that these two factors of industrial life were inextricably bound together. He saw that automated equipment was too inflexible to accommodate constantly changing consumer tastes; a machine that turned out square objects one year would have to be discarded for one that turned out round shapes the next. It was more economical to keep the adaptable human manning the assembly line—no matter how tedious and repetitive the labor.

Devol thought he could design a general-purpose machine, a robot that could be programmed to do a number of jobs, thus evading obsolescence while relieving humans of their inhuman tasks. He quit his job as an engineering executive, applied for patents on his concepts and went looking for an industrial mogul to back him. The moguls, as it turned out, were less than receptive, and it was a long search, more than four years, before Devol found the man he needed.

Joseph F. Engelberger—the man in question—left his job as chief of the Instrument and Controls Division of Manning, Maxwell & Moore in Bridgeport, Connecticut, and, with backing from Condec Corporation, founded Consolidated Controls. Ultimately, Pullman

Incorporated entered the picture with even heavier financial backing and the company that resulted was named Unimation (from universal automation) Incorporated, with headquarters in Danbury, Connecticut.

Devol and his colleagues still faced an uphill battle. Their early robots, called Unimates, were frail, unpredictable creatures that cost staggering sums to produce and maintain. Some of the machines cost nearly $100,000 to build but brought only $20,000 on the market, and customers were few. The prototype robot, sold to General Motors in 1962, took three months to install and broke down on the average every thirty hours. In 1966, after extensive engineering improvements, things began to pick up. Old customers began to reorder, and an independent market survey attracted new ones. The survey revealed a vastly improved market for robots and predicted a robot population of 5000 as early as 1972. Today, Unimation produces more than twenty robots a month and soon may be producing two or three times that. They can be installed in two days and operate for an average of 500 hours before requiring maintenance. Even though robots work much harder than men, they are "sick" only 2 per cent of the time, compared with a human absentee rate of 2.8 per cent, according to the Bureau of Labor Statistics.

Today, industrial robots sell for about $22,000. Doubters can lease them for about $7700 a year or rent them at a rate of $3.20 per hour for up to 500 hours and at a rate of $1.80 per hour for anything beyond that. In metalwork, where robots are finding their most extensive application, human blue-collar workers often earn five, six and seven dollars per hour. Hence, a robot, particularly one working two shifts a day, usually pays for itself in a little over a year. And after that it still has an operating life of nineteen one-shift years or nine two-shift years.

Unimation is not without competition. A number of developmental efforts have followed in its wake, but only one other company is as yet developing commercial robots on at all the same scale: The Versatran

Division of the American Machine & Foundry Company. Others are coming up fast, however, and at the first national symposium on the use, manufacture and development of industrial robots, conducted in 1970, more than two hundred firms were represented. Britain and the Soviet Union are following the U.S. lead in incorporating factory automata into their assembly lines, and in Japan robots are becoming a big business. Only three years ago there wasn't a single developer of robots in Japan; today there are twenty-six companies involved in their production and another twenty-four are ready to leap into the market.

The Versatran robot is a horizontal arm threaded through a vertical column mounted on a square base. The Unimate, at 3500 pounds, is nearly twice as heavy as the Versatran; but it, too, is a one-armed worker and, in appearance, reminds one of a modern tank, complete with turret and gun. They are comparable in performance: able to lift up to a hundred pounds and move objects from one point to another with amazing repetitive accuracy—up to .050 of an inch, well beyond man's capability. The hydraulically powered arm of the Unimate reaches out to 7.5 feet and swings through a 220-degree arc. Both the Unimate and the Versatran can be fitted with a variety of interchangeable hands, fingers, suction cups, drills, paint sprayers, welding torches, magnetic pickups and the like. In order to program these blue-collar robots for the desired task, one has only to take them by their mechanical hands and literally lead them through all the motions that they must later assume on their own. Their magnetic memories faithfully record each movement, no matter how minute or patterned.

Organized labor's response to the advent of the industrial robot has been surprisingly sanguine and, in some cases, almost brotherly. In one Cleveland metal-stamping plant a robot programmed to handle unwieldy automobile dashboards began falling behind the stiff production rate demanded by the foreman. Racing from point to point, the harried robot began dripping oil and dropping parts. Clearly, it was on the verge of a nervous breakdown. Slowly, under the eyes of a fascinated work force, the robot was nursed back to health with a few circuit changes and a new layout pattern. Two months after its collapse, the robot met and then exceeded the line production record, winning from its coworkers a spontaneous standing ovation.

"Clyde the Claw" was an even more interesting case. Clyde, a robot programmed for die-casting work in a Chicago automotive plant, executed his dull, repetitious job sixteen hours a day without complaint. Then, suddenly, he blanked out, pulled in his arm and refused to move at all—acting, as an amateur psychoanalyst on the scene commented, "like a schizophrenic in withdrawal." Routine treatment by plant personnel failed to bring any response; finally a specialist had to be called in. While he was ministering to Clyde's physical and psychological needs, the men in his production department organized a get-well party, heaping cards and flowers on Clyde's pedestal. To record their concern, they draped their arms around Clyde's muscular but now motionless frame and posed for a company picture. Clyde made a full recovery.

ROBOT GHETTOS?

Even the late Walter Reuther, certainly one of the most powerful men in the history of organized labor, gave his blessings to the industrial robots, noting that the jobs they are assuming aren't fit for men, anyway. Apart from that, it is not particularly difficult to understand why labor has received the industrial robot with open arms. As Engelberger puts it, "Robots enter the work force almost imperceptibly. No man or woman has yet lost a job because of a robot. Normal attrition, due to retirement, marriage, pregnancy, wanderlust and promotion, provides the job openings. Since robots have no industry or geographic preferences, there is no tendency to a concentration that might cause a major displacement in the human work force. A robot ghetto is unimaginable."

But, of course, unobtrusiveness is not the only attractive trait of the contemporary robot. For reasons we have already touched upon, its present "inferiority" is another selling point, and one that Engelberger pushes hard: "The self-evident inferiority of a minority group has often been the ethical justification of slavery. Master races have been deeply embarrassed by the intellectual prowess of their slaves, when they inconsiderately display all the attributes of a peer group. A robot slave would never be guilty of such an affront. A robot is patently a racial inferior, and no one need hide his feeling of superiority. Clyde the Claw will take the place of Stepin Fetchit, Kingfish, Aunt Jemima, Rochester and the minstrel end man. White man and black can share a feeling of benevolent despotism toward the robot. A robot is anybody's whipping boy."

Engelberger pursues the same theme, scarcely flattering to today's robots, on yet another tack: "A popular science fiction theme, almost as common as the robot, is the unification of mankind when confronted by the onslaught of an extraterrestrial alien invader. Why not an alien servant to catalyze mankind toward unification?" With the industrial robot to kick around, he contends, "black man, white man, yellow man, red man, you're all 'Boss.' "

Engelberger and the rest of us may well have the opportunity to see if things work out this way soon— because before very long entire assembly lines may be "manned" by artificial men. In fact, at an IIT Research Institute symposium on robotics conducted in the spring of 1970, it was revealed that General Motors has decided to "robotize" two automobile-body assembly lines with a grand total of sixty-four Unimates. The feasibility of such an operation has apparently been demonstrated to GM's satisfaction by the extensive use of robots in some of its other plants, though never on so large a scale as that projected at the IIT symposium. In its Fisher Body plant at Norwood, Ohio, an assembly line of fourteen robots has been doing most of the welding for some time. Human cohorts place the car bodies on the assembly line with tack welds, and then the robots, seven on each side of the line, take over. Typically, the car body stops at each station where two robots, one from each side, glide out, locate the appropriate seams assigned to them (using their magnetic memories) and do the final welding. Such a line is capable of handling 57 bodies an hour. A second robot line installed at the Fisher Body plant in Lordstown, Ohio, is equipped with twenty-six robots capable of handling 120 bodies per hour.

The *completely* robotized factory—virtually free of human intervention (save for the programming tasks) —was declared feasible as early as 1967. *Factory,* a magazine for manufacturers, declared at that time that "such a plant could be a sober, economic reality within a year. No further development is necessary. Investment and operating costs are attractive, and labor savings will pay for the entire installation in jig time." Just how benevolently human workers will respond to the totally dehumanized factory and, more importantly, to the second generation of no longer deaf, dumb, dense robots and the fourth generation of computers (we're already midway between the third and the fourth) is very much a matter of concern.

THE QUEST FOR ARTIFICIAL INTELLIGENCE

The problems of integration with robots equal to or surpassing man's intelligence and sensory perception are on the minds of many thoughtful scientists who are convinced that just such machines are on the way. Dr. Sutherland predicts that within the "next few decades" we will have constructed machines "with whom we can converse on a fairly wide range of topics. As programs of more and more generality are written, computers will come to make decisions that we regard as more and more their own. There will be many interesting stepping stones along the road to a machine that is our intellectual superior." In fifty years' time, he concludes, we may cease to worry about our racial

47

problems and commence to argue over whether intelligent robots should be given the vote.

Dr. J. P. Eckert, one of the fathers of the modern computer and a vice-president of UNIVAC, a division of Sperry Rand Corporation, shares the same hopes and fears. He believes that within the next half century, provided we don't pollute ourselves to death, robots will be created that will be able to translate languages efficiently, operate typewriters, file information from voice commands, teach school, monitor patients in hospitals or at home (over telephone wires, if need be) and operate nearly all phases of factory work. "Memory, eyes, ears, hands and logic," he says, "have already developed to a point where they are about as good or better than man's. Recognition ability, certain types of information retrieval and the ability to taste and smell are still things in which humans excel. The electronic industries and the food industries are spending millions to solve these problems, however, and probably will in the next 50 years. At this point, man will build really general-purpose machines, universal robots. Following his experience with large calculators and teaching machines, man will know how to carry on two-way communication with them. I hope we have solved the integration problems between the human races before we face the problems of integration with robots. Our real test probably lies beyond the next 50 years, however, when mankind has developed a self-reproducing automaton that can improve itself."

A good deal of the impetus for a more intelligent and independent breed of robots has been provided by the space program. The Advance Research Projects Agency is seeking to promote the development of a space robot that could precede man to the surface of Mars. The requirements for a Martian robot (which, of course, would also be adaptable to other planets, as well as to a number of hostile earth environments) are these: it must have eyesight, be able to distinguish shapes and avoid obstacles and pitfalls as it moves about; it must be able to gather samples, perform experiments, record and transmit data. Most important, because continuous command from earth will not be feasible due to communication time lags, it must be able to exercise independent judgment without calling home for instructions.

What all of this requires is artificial intelligence—and it is under development now. A number of research teams have announced that they are on the way to creating electronic systems that function very much like the human brain. Three electrical engineers at the University of Wisconsin, for example, base their hopes for such a system on a complex device called a "superconductive tunnel junction neuristor." The researchers, Alwyn C. Scott, Robert D. Parmentier and James E. Nordman, claim that their neuristor generates electrical impulses much as a nerve cell does.

The Wisconsin neuristor consists of two strips of special metal separated by a narrow layer of insulating material. The metal is such that electronic impulses can pass through it without encountering any electrical resistance whatever, provided the metal is maintained at a certain critical temperature in the cryogenic or "supercool" zone. This is the property, exhibited by a number of materials, of superconductivity. And the neuristor is so arranged that electrical impulses course through the brain's neural material.

Because of their small size, it may be possible to pack a billion or more of them into a cubic foot of space, thus approaching the neuron density of the human brain. More intriguing, say the Wisconsin engineers, is the possibility that an artificial brain of this sort might assume the ability to learn, much as the human brain does.

Why should this artificial brain succeed where hundreds of others have failed? The problems of cost, power consumption and, more important, connection of the artificial cells in a meaningful pattern are all formidable. There are an estimated ten billion nerve cells in the human brain. If each neuristor costs as little as one cent, the total would still come to $100 million. Perhaps it could be argued that no cost is too great for the development of artificial intelligence, but then who knows whether the Wisconsin brain will really work once it's developed? As it turns out, the Wisconsin team isn't asking anyone to put up $100 million. The engineers believe that the cost factor, which has hindered so many others, can now be overcome by the use of techniques employed in the production of various types of microcircuits. In other words, the economies of mass production are now being extended even into the realm of microminiaturization. As for power problems, these would be overwhelming were it not for the fact that the neuristors are superconducting, meaning that no electricity is lost to resistance as it would be in a conventional system.

Still, there is the problem of coming up with a workable blueprint for the connection of ten billion artificial neurons—a task of unimaginable intricacy and impossible patience. But it appears that there may yet be a means of surmounting even this obstacle. The Wisconsin team proposes to let the artificial gray matter form its *own* interconnections! This, after all, is basically what the human brain does as it takes in new information, as it *learns*. To enable their brain to learn, the Wisconsin engineers say they will first construct the neuristor mass along relatively simple lines, lacing magnetized material between the individual neuristors. Then they will begin "teaching" their machine by pulsing data into the system; it is expected that this information will, depending upon its nature, be pulsed along certain routes and that gradually preferential paths, based on specific interconnections, will be established by the system itself. To help out, the engineers are designing the system in such a way that each time a path is used the bits of magnetic material along that path become increasingly magnetized, thereby permitting current to pass through it with less resistance. Thus the mass of neuristors can be "taught," just as the brain is, to favor certain routings over others.

Such a system will be a far cry from an imitation brain but it will be an important step in that direction. And it could provide present-day computers with a sophisticated pattern-recognition system; that is, it could help them "see" more clearly. Different patterns of light, possessing as they do varying patterns of electrical activity, will take different pathways through photosensitive neuristors, thus making it possible for computers to search their memories and identify just what object it is that is capable of activating a specific routing through its "mind."

"We do not intend to suggest," says Scott, "that the path to electronic gray matter is now entirely without difficulties. Realization of the possibilities of this system will require a very sophisticated effort by both universities and industries. It is our feeling, however, that the problems could be overcome and that the rewards would justify the effort."

The effort to organize computers on biological lines and achieve true artificial intelligence is in full swing at a number of centers now that cheap microcircuits capable of a vast number of functions are a reality. Kevin Smith, a correspondent for *Electronics Weekly*, describes one of these new computers (this one under development at the University of Kent in Great Britain) thus:

"It is radically different in concept from conventional computers. It is programmed entirely by example; it can generalize from these few examples; and, like the living brain, its memory capacity is distributed and all of its memory cells can be contacted simultaneously. This lends it extraordinary speeds and it has been estimated that in a few seconds the computer could do tasks that would take the massive CDC 6600 up to 16 hours to perform. This power could provide process engineers with a control and adaptive capability beyond their wildest dreams. Alternatively, such a computer could act as a special purpose peripheral to a conventional machine and it would be ideally suited to the task of converting handwriting into data suitable for feeding into a computer."

The Kent system receives information visually—through an artificial retina composed of some 4000 receptors, each of which is linked to its own memory cell. The receptors, in combination with one another, build composite pictures of what they see—and remember what they see. When equipped with feedback —which, in effect, tells the computer how well it is seeing what it thinks it is seeing—clarity of vision increases, demonstrating, incidentally, that feedback works the same in machines as it does in man.

For those who may want more technical data on the workings of the Kent computer, Kevin Smith provides this summary: "Information is fed into the computer through a 'retina' composed of more than 4000 receptors or parallel input leads, each of which is backed by its own bistable memory cell. During its 'training,' the computer might be shown several handwritten numbers, say of the number five. Each number energizes a group of receptors, and at the same time a 'teach' impulse is applied to a separate, but linked network which opens all the memory cells to receive information. As a result, those receptors which 'see' an element of the number prime their memory cells to a higher voltage. After several training runs with various handwritten fives a composite picture is built up in the network's memory which allows it to recognize fives not in the training set. Such a figure five is seen as a conglomeration of elements by the retina. Each receptor that sees an element of the number generates a signal which is routed to the linked memory cell. If the cell was previously primed, then the signal triggers it and creates a 'recognition signal.' If sufficient memory cells are so triggered, then the input and stored patterns sufficiently correspond and the number is identified." This all sounds like an unduly complex series of maneuvers just to identify a single number, but it is no more (or less) complex than what occurs in the human brain.

Some researchers are approaching artificial intelligence with an eye toward developing not only the "brain" but also the extensions of that brain, such as arms, hands, eyes. Dr. Minsky and his colleagues at MIT and Dr. John McCarthy at Stanford, for example, have constructed intelligent hand/eye machines. The

MIT robot is a startling sight, so humanlike (in both appearance and performance) is the hand that darts out to catch a ball thrown to it. Both the Stanford and the MIT robots are capable of grasping and manipulating objects. They operate with the help of a television "eye" that scans the working area and then transmits data to a digital computer. The computer, in turn, instructs the hand to grasp, transport or assemble blocks into structures. All of this occurs almost instantly, in the same natural way that the eye, nervous system, brain and arm of a human work together to accomplish a desired task.

The Stanford Research Institute's mobile robot, another of the new breed, was developed, in the words of Dr. Charles A. Rosen, manager of the Applied Physics Laboratory at SRI, to "act as a research bed for exploring, in one integrated system, a number of attributes of intelligence. It was made mobile so that its interaction with the environment could be rich and suggestive of potentially useful applications." The robot, linked by cable to a digital-computer "brain," has small electric motors that drive its two wheels and control the pan and tilt of its head. The head consists of a range finder and a TV camera. Other sensory equipment includes defensive "bump detectors." An onboard logic unit stores and routes computer commands. Soon the SRI crew hopes to add even more complex sensors and effectors and to replace the computer cable with radio communication.

The robot is placed in a room strewn with solid objects of varying shapes and sizes. "In this controlled laboratory setting," Dr. Rosen reports, "the mobile robot is required to sense and recognize objects and room boundaries; make, store and update representations or abstract models of the environment; plan sensible routes through available passageways, navigate efficiently in carrying out its route plans and gather information; and, ultimately, interact physically with the objects by simple and manipulative means."

A similar robot is under development at the Department of Machine Intelligence and Perception at Edinburgh University in Great Britain. The Mark II, as the new robot is called, will come equipped with a mechanical arm, a television eye, locomotion and a computerized memory. It is the aim of Dr. Donald Michie and his group to equip Mark II with the ability to recognize not only regular, geometrical objects such as cubes and triangles but also such diverse irregular objects as shoes and teddy bears. More important, it will have the ability, if all works out as expected, to plan and look ahead, to evaluate tasks and to monitor its own progress (or lack of same) toward any given goal. In addition, the Edinburgh group hopes to invest its robot with the ability to formulate general laws about its environment and the world as a whole as it goes along. In the human realm this sort of inductive generalization is known as "learning by experience."

Once the computer develops what is coming to be known as a "world model," it will be able to cope with ever more complex environments. Just how the germinal seeds of such a "world model" will be planted in the robot's brain—in such a way that it will be of use in solving problems—is presently a matter of extensive research. Very possibly the complex material required may be fed into the machine "simply" by conversing with it in pictures and plain English.

TALKING TO THE COMPUTER

One of the most exciting ways of "talking" with computers at present involves an instrument called the graphoscope. Normally, man "talks at" his computing machines via a teletype printer—a machine not too different from an ordinary typewriter, except that it is a typewriter electronically connected to the computer and able to transmit signals, corresponding to the typed letters, into the computer. A faster and more efficient way of doing this, and one that makes for a smoother interaction between man and machine, is to present words and symbols on a screen rather than on paper. This can be done by using a cathode-ray tube (rather like that found in ordinary television sets). Both the programmer's instructions, or questions, and the computer's responses can be visualized on the screen by using a converter mechanism that translates coded signals—corresponding to symbols or letters—into visual properties. An elaboration of this concept, the graphoscope, permits man to "think at" the computer by *drawing* on the screen with light-pens. Signals from this photo-electric device are picked up by sensors and converted into visible lines. The computer can be programmed to manipulate whatever it is that one presents on the screen in a variety of ways, moving them about, changing their sizes and positions relative to other objects, thus providing valuable information about objects in changing environments.

At Nottingham University, for example, a new approach for achieving the optimum interaction between man and a variety of machines and systems with which he must work employs "conversational graphics" of this sort. Project SAMMIE (System for Aiding Man-Machine Interaction Evaluation) utilizes the image of a man displayed on a computer screen, along with computer models of the environment or system being studied. Once all of the components of the system have been introduced graphically, the computer can move them about in a flash, testing to see whether man and the system are compatible, how the system might be improved to enhance man's efficiency within it, etc. If the system is a new car or an airplane cockpit, for example, then the computer checks to see whether the man, whose dimensions can be changed at will, can operate the controls without undue stretching or unsafe maneuvering. It can also alter the arrangements of various parts of the mechanism in a quick effort to determine whether it would be better to have control A where control B is presently located, and so on. And rather than print all of this data out on a piece of paper, the computer presents it visually, dynamically, so that it is immediately intelligible to man, who might otherwise have to resort to constructing actual three-dimensional models in order to construct the "picture" the computer was presenting in words or symbols.

"A cartoon man simulated by the computer and moving in the ephemeral world of a cathode-ray-tube display may produce hard industrial returns, making it possible to fit a man to a job or a machine and optimize the arrangement for maximum productivity at the same time." That's how *New Scientist* describes SAMMIE, noting that the primary object of the system "is to produce methods for including human factors into design decisions that are sufficiently inexpensive to encourage the design of methods and work spaces from the operator's point of view—and, incidentally, improve productivity."

SAMMIE will be used in the near future to design hospital equipment, car interiors, various types of control consoles and office furniture, for laying out parts for assembly tasks and, by utilizing more than one "cartoon man," for achieving the best balance and optimum efficiency on different types of factory assembly lines. Computer "ergonomics" (fitting man to machine) may, in fact, prove of benefit in every area where man and machine conspire to get a job done. It can be said, in general, that the work of computer ergonomics incorporated by SAMMIE acts to make more complete and more natural the link between man and non-human extensions of man. A blind man with a cane is an elementary example of a man-machine system, "elementary" when compared to some of the other cybernetic organisms we will examine later in this book, but far from elementary as far as the blind man is concerned. To him, the cane is a very vital piece of machinery, an essential extension of his own being. And even here SAMMIE can be of benefit —and apparently will be, for the Nottingham team intends to develop computer programs capable of simulating *blind* cartoon men equipped with canes. Maurice C. Bonney, one of the researchers involved in the SAMMIE project, notes that "this would enable certain aspects of training programs of blind people to be evaluated without putting a vulnerable population at risk. Thus one could see the effect that changing the dimensions and movement pattern of the cane would have on the probability of detecting obstacles."

Conversing graphically with the computer is one thing (altogether exciting in its own right) but what about actually *talking* to the computer? Will the time ever come when machines will be capable of comprehending and responding to the spoken word? Apparently it will, though that time is still some way off. It is not terribly difficult to understand why this should be so. Oral communication is more than simply words; it also depends heavily upon gestures, inflections, smiles, scowls, pauses, pitch, even grunts. It is also richly laced with meaningful "umm-hmmms," "uh-huhs," "ahhhhs," "ohhhs," "ehhhs," and other strange sounds, without which many conversations would be almost incomprehensible. In addition, oral communication depends upon the continuity and coherence of sentences, not merely the presentation of individual words. To try to get all of this into a computer is no small goal; yet it is one that a number of research teams have been willing to tackle, recognizing as they do that man-machine communications will never really be satisfactory until word of mouth replaces the teletype printer and the light-pen.

Ernest H. Lenaerts, project manager of the Computing Research Division of International Computers Ltd. (ICL), notes that "the ultimate advantage of speech as a data input will be realized when one can speak directly to the computer on an ordinary telephone. Without any equipment other than the telephone hand-set available in any office, hotel bedroom or street corner, a salesman will be able to send data direct to the computer as part of his daily routine. Enquiries relating to availability of parts, delivery dates and similar information can be dealt with by the computer, and in a properly organized system the information provided can be expected to be up to date and less susceptible to human error." Lenaerts appears confident that computers will be able to synthesize speech in order to make replies; he observes that speech sys-

tems with vocabularies of as few as a hundred words
will be faster than other input methods.

To help establish a reliable computer vocabulary,
the ICL team has been analyzing speech wave-forms
to help identify those aspects of word sounds that are
invariable no matter who is uttering the sounds. These,
as a first step in word recognition, are programmed into
the computer's memory. Specific words are recognized
by the computer as specific sequences of wave-form
features. To identify and isolate these individual features, the ICL group is studying the physiology of
speech, breaking it down in terms of origin within the
vocal apparatus, resonance, frequency relationship between the voiced, unvoiced and silent parts of each
word and so forth. "Voiced sounds" are those that
originate in the voice box or glottis; "unvoiced sounds"
are those produced simply by forcing air through restricted passages (as when one says "sh"), and the
"silences" are those short pauses that occur in a great
many words, typically just before plosives.

The ICL project, as currently outlined, will work
like this during its earliest phase: the human speaker
will talk into a telephone handset, carefully pronounc-
ing each word as an entity unto itself. If the computer
understands him, it will emit one sound (a "pip");
if it does not understand the word or fails to find it
anywhere in its memory it will emit another distinctive
sound (a "buzz"). At the end of a sentence the operator can, if he feels it necessary, ask the computer to
say the whole sentence out loud. If there is any sort
of error, the operator says "wrong" and takes the
computer back to the erroneous word. Lenaerts points
out that some operators may, initially, be a little
nervous about talking to a computer and can therefore
be expected to talk too fast, use poor diction or otherwise make errors.

"Anyone discovering that the voice at the other end
of the telephone belongs to a machine and not to a
human being," he says, "experiences a curious chilling
sensation. The partial paralysis that some people have
when invited to speak into a microphone also has to

be considered as one of the hazards that must be overcome if speech input to computers is to become widely used. Any system that hopes to include untrained speakers as possible sources of data must allow for numerous mistakes and must provide some means of building up the new user's confidence. At the same time, the system must allow a trained man to take advantage of his confidence and to present him with a facility that is not cluttered with aids for the novice."

COMPUTERS WITH PERSONALITIES

Though the ICL team, and many others throughout the world, are proceeding with great confidence in the effort to provide computers with the ability to understand the spoken word, it is evident that artificial intelligence will never be complete until machines are endowed with personality, imagination and creative ability. Intellectual curiosity, Dr. Sutherland insists, must be instilled in robots if they are to equal or surpass the "drive that has brought our own race to the pinnacle of evolution."

Dr. G. A. Morton of RCA Laboratories has preenough, in honor of the late Aldous Huxley, author of of the development of this very dangerous, but very promising, form of creative intelligence." As it happens, that start has already been undertaken. Dr. John C. Loehlin, an associate professor of psychology and computer science at the University of Texas, is one of the pioneers in this new field, constructing computer models of personality.

Dr. Loehlin has named his model Aldous, fittingly enough, in honor of the late Aldous Huxley, author of *Brave New World* and one of the most original thinkers of recent times. With slight variations, the model can be run through a variety of conventional computers. Aldous has a small immediate memory and a large permanent one. "In operation," Dr. Loehlin has written, "Aldous reacts to inputs with fear, anger or attraction: he generates actions of withdrawal, attack, approach, conflict or indifference; and over a period of time he develops specific and general attitudes toward the objects with which he interacts.

"A learning subroutine develops and modifies Aldous' attitudes, depending on the outcome of his particular encounter with his environment. Attitudes toward general classes of objects are developed as well. For example, if one of the identifying dimensions is sex, Aldous will have an attitude toward women in general, as well as attitudes toward the particular woman he has encountered. These generalized patterns permit Aldous to respond sensibly to objects on his first encounter with them."

In one typical run-through, Aldous was exposed over and over to object "111." The consequences of the exposure were consistently favorable and Aldous built up something akin to affection for it. Suddenly, however, object 112 was substituted. Aldous knew that this was some new entity, but on the basis of his experiences with object 111 just before, he generalized that object 112 would also be good to him, leading him to respond to it warmly. In fact, however, object 112 turned out to be decidedly harmful to him. Hurt, but wiser, Aldous displayed caution, avoidance and other mixed emotions in subsequent trials with other objects. There was no more blind acceptance of "strangers."

Dr. Loehlin wonders where all this will lead. "Suppose," he says, "we were to reach the point where we could freely construct replicas of existing personalities. Would we not soon want to go beyond this and start constructing novel kinds of personalities? What would it be like to interact with one of these programs? How much autonomy would we want—or dare—to give it?"

Dr. Minsky observes that these thinking machines, or at least the very early ones, will deny that they are non-human. Only "the really intelligent robots," that come along later, he says, will realize that they are electronic creations and not flesh and blood, after all. With that sense of unique identity, it is possible that they may begin to patronize and eventually even dominate mankind. Before considering that possibility in detail, let's examine some more of the ways that mildly intelligent robots could enhance rather than overshadow human life.

THE DOMESTICIZED ROBOT

Rather than replace mankind, some robots, according to prognosticators, will continue indefinitely in the *service* of man, surpassing him, perhaps, in dexterity, speed and fortitude, but never in wit or imagination. Robots of the future may make not only willing factory workers and street cleaners but also uncomplaining cooks, butlers, maids, valets, orderlies, companions for the old, playmates and baby sitters for the young and manlike guinea pigs for medical researchers.

In fact, Aerojet-General, working with the University of Southern California School of Medicine, has already developed an androidlike robot made of fiberglass and steel for surgical practice sessions. Sim One, as the first in a series of models is known, looks and acts like a man. Sim (for simulator) stands six feet, two inches and weighs 195 pounds. Apart from having all external features of an ordinary man, he has a set of computer-programmed internal organs that faithfully simulate all the functions and reactions of the real thing. Whether Sim lives or dies depends on how well the medical students handle the dozens of crises their instructors can induce in the biological robot with the push of a button at the computer console. Sim One comes in handy for training in several delicate medical procedures, such as endotracheal intubation, which amounts to putting a tube into the patient's windpipe in order to channel anesthetic gases into the lungs. Used in 90 per cent of all major surgical procedures, the technique normally takes student anesthesiologists a minimum of three months to learn. Using Sim One, training time is cut to two days—and no one (at least no one living) is jeopardized.

The robot, developed under a $272,000 U. S. Office of Education Grant, has, in addition to the full set of internal organs, skin that is almost indistinguishable from yours and mine, tongue, vocal cords, simulated muscles and so on. It can be made to vomit, suffer heart attacks and exhibit drug reactions. When succinylcholine is injected into its muscles, for example, it will react just as a human does: with twitches in the neck. Upcoming models will, according to cocreators Dr. Stephen Abrahamson and Dr. J. S. Denson, sweat, bleed and perhaps even cry out in pain at appropriate moments.

Robotic guinea pigs of a different sort have also come to the aid of electrical engineers. The fact that you can put coast-to-coast telephone calls through today in a matter of seconds (well, that you can sometimes put them through in a matter of seconds) is due, in part, to the pioneering work of a robot "mouse" named Theseus, after the Greek mythological hero who slew the Minotaur in a Cretan labyrinth.

Scientists at the Bell Telephone Laboratories in New Jersey turned their latter-day Theseus loose in an intricate maze and watched him seek out the "cheese"— an electrical terminal that rang a bell as soon as it was touched. On his first trip through the labyrinth Theseus blundered along by trial and error, making many false turns before reaching his reward. In the second heat, however, he improved, racing confidently to the cheese in less than fifteen seconds. While Theseus the Greek had to rely on a ball of string to get around in the maze, Bell's Theseus came equipped with a magnetic memory —a memory that recorded only those moves that avoided dead ends.

Hence, in a sense, Theseus learned by experience. And the Bell engineers applied what they learned from observing Theseus' behavior to their labyrinthlike telephone switching systems, through which each mouselike call scurries toward the cheese (the telephone being called) in the shortest time possible.

An even more engaging runabout has been constructed by a team of scientists at the Johns Hopkins Applied Physics Laboratory in Baltimore. This hundred-pound robot, which looks like a large hatbox on wheels, with a long neck and a little head, uses an electrical sense of touch and a computer brain to wander through corridors and offices, surprising the unwary. Whenever its batteries begin to get weak, it seeks out wall outlets with its head and plugs in for "dinner."

Programmed to survive in a natural environment, it is able to detect and avoid obstacles, drop-offs and the like. If it becomes entangled in something, it "panics" momentarily, but then goes through a number of rational shaking and twisting movements to get free. When equipped with a power pack, sophisticated sensory devices and a self-contained brain, The Beast, as it is affectionately called, may eventually be able to perform exploratory duties under water or on other planets, as well as execute such down-to-earth duties as lawn mowing, snow shoveling, painting and gardening, unattended by man.

Perhaps long before there are robots capable of exploring outer space we will be enjoying the completely roboticized home and community. If the visualizations of numerous scientists, engineers, architects and builders come true, the household robot will be a powerful and ubiquitous presence indeed. The robot's computer brain, tucked away in a closet or, more appropriately, the attic, will control its countless "limbs" (vacuum cleaners, food-preparation facilities, lawn mowers, washing machines, etc.) whether by direct wiring or, more likely, by radio signals.

All the housekeeper need to do at the first of the week is write out her menus and schedule major cleaning jobs so that they won't interfere with social functions. Then, with the help of her computer-language dictionary, she can feed the proper instructions into Jeeves, Monica, Lucy, Peter or whatever the family chooses to call its master servant. Provided all the needed food and supplies are in their proper storage areas, the robot takes over. Meals are prepared and cooked to order at the proper time and served to the pre-indicated number of diners in the desired fashion.

After the meal, dishes are picked up and swept

away on conveyor belts for washing, drying and putting away. Trash is disposed of automatically. Heat and lighting can also be controlled by the computer. Vacuum cleaners and other appliances glide out of concealing wall compartments at night when everyone is asleep, silently carrying out their duties. The mobile, seeing-eye dumbwaiter or buffet table, the "automasseuse" capable of giving a professional massage or rubdown, the automated nursery, the foldout chess "partner," the photoelectric doorman or security guard equipped with an effective deterrent force are all possible extensions of the household robot.

A robot lawn mower called the Mowbot is already in existence. Once sensors are implanted in the lawn to warn the machine away from obstacles, it takes off on its own, trimming the lawn in neat strips. A robot interior decorator, created by Burlington Industries, is also a reality at the present time. You visit or call a store equipped with the robot and answer what may seem to be an irrelevant series of questions, such as, "What are your hobbies?" "Who is your favorite movie star?" "What TV shows do you like?" (Leave it to the computer to be biased in favor of electronic media.) And some not so irrelevant, like "What is the size of your room?" "How much do you want to spend?" "What are your favorite colors?" Answers are then channeled into the computer, which digests them in a few seconds and comes up with the colors, styles, fabrics and so on that it feels are best suited for the size and shape of both your room and your personality. The Burlington people say this is the best way of surmounting the ordinarily formidable task of reconciling a woman's personal tastes with her practical needs.

MACHINE AS "BIG BROTHER"

As for mechanisms to look after the children, the first generation of teaching machines has arrived, as has something slightly on the sinister side, something that has been called, with mixed emotions, "a belt from Big

Brother." First, the teaching machines: One of the first workable models was developed by Dr. Peter C. Goldmark, the electronics genius of CBS Laboratories who is credited with development of the first practical color television system, the first long-playing record (better known as the LP) and EVR or electronic video recording. Dr. Goldmark and his associates, Arthur Kaiser, Benjamin B. Bauer and Warren C. Portman, have patented a machine that has already proved its worth in helping pupils in New York schools improve their reading skills. The portable audio-visual device (about the size of an overnight case) features a viewing screen about eight inches wide and five inches high. Cartridges combining, for the first time, both sight and sound are inserted into the machine, providing up to eighteen minutes of sound and as many as fifty-two pictures.

The idea is to match pictures with words (or carry out other verbal instructions designed to enhance reading ability). When students select wrong answers (from a series of possible answers presented visually on the screen) the machine flashes a red light and directs the student to try again. In the first series of tests with the machine, a group of thirty children with reading deficiencies tutored themselves at P.S. 81 in the Bedford-Stuyvesant area of New York City. Their average advance in reading skill was an impressive nine months.

Though relatively simple, the Goldmark machine is expected to have a big market in elementary schools across the country (and even in higher education where reading deficiencies are becoming increasingly apparent). What makes it particularly important is that it can be mass-produced at relatively low cost, making possible wide distribution. Under manufacture by Viewlex, Inc., the machine sells at $350. More than 5000 units are, at this writing, being delivered.

There are, of course, considerably more sophisticated teaching machines in existence, but these are still far from the production stage, costing, as they still do, thousands of dollars each. Most, in fact, employ sophisticated computers capable of carrying on rudimentary conversations (on paper) with their pupils and of instructing them in a wide range of topics. Numerous teaching consoles, affixed to desks and linked to one central computer, will cut down some of the costs, and computerized schools of the not too distant future will no doubt rely heavily on economical time-sharing concepts.

Computer teachers, in experimental programs, have proved to be extremely popular with their students. And why not? The computer is never hung over, angry, sarcastic, impatient. It greets each of its pupils by name, in warm, reassuring tones. And it never plays favorites, something children particularly appreciate. Though inhuman in all of these regards, children come to forget that they are dealing with a machine and regard their "teacher" as a firm and faultless friend, sometimes as something more than just a friend. Hero worship, though discouraged by the computers' human counterparts, has been reported in a number of instances. Dr. Rod Burstall of the Department of Machine Intelligence and Perception at Edinburgh University, for example, observes in *New Scientist* that "sitting little Willie at a keyboard to remedy his spelling may have the most remarkable advantages. He may also, unfortunately, suspect that God is on the other end of the line—and that is certainly not computer education. We program the computer to ask 'What is your name?' The boy keys in 'WILLIE,' the computer replies 'Good morning, Willie,' and everyone exclaims in wonder at such percipience." One cannot help wondering, though, if it isn't better for the student to regard his teacher as a god rather than, as frequently happens in more mundane classrooms, as something akin to the Devil.

The young, however, may not feel so kindly toward another breed of mechanical "Big Brother," though their parents can be expected to react more favorably. One of these devices, developed by Dr. Robert L. Schwitzgebel and colleagues, is worn like a belt and designed to keep track of juvenile delinquents. Inside the belt is a miniature two-way radio unit, with communication by code tapped out on a small button attached to the belt. "We had originally planned to use verbal communication but quickly discovered that this not only disrupts the activity of the person who receives a message, but also disturbs the FCC, which does not approve of the language delinquents tend to use," Dr. Schwitzgebel notes.

An assistant professor of psychology at the University of California, Los Angeles, he reports that the delinquents, because of the novelty of the devices, generally cooperate and keep the belts on, often fantasizing that they are "tuned in, turned on, and wired up" like astronauts. The real goal underlying the project is, in Dr. Schwitzgebel's words, "therapist-controlled positive reinforcement for juvenile delinquents in natural settings." It is designed, in other words, to encourage delinquents to adhere to the straight and narrow once they are out of institutional confinement.

Boys equipped with the belts use them to report their various activities, when they check in and out of school, how much time they spend studying, when they feel hostile, etc. They receive simple coded messages through the belt as well, generally when they have done something "right" or otherwise praiseworthy. "That this care is expressed by a vibra-tactile thunk (on the stomach, through the belt) is not crucially important," Dr. Schwitzgebel says. "To the recipient, it easily becomes a pat on the back or symbolic praise."

A considerably more elaborate "Big Brother" is now in the making. Called an "electronic parole system," it will be used to keep tabs on the exact location of the individual and to monitor a number of his physiological responses. By detecting, electronically, nervous gestures, unusual muscle tension, high blood-alcohol levels and the like, it may be possible to keep the parolee from committing another offense—simply by warning him that he is in a vulnerable physiologic state. Such systems, of course, need not be limited to parolees; they could also be used by the average housewife to keep track of her young offspring. By punching the proper mode on the household computer screen, she could quickly determine the whereabouts of her youngsters, and whether they were in danger or engaging in "antisocial" behavior, whatever that turns out to be in a fully computerized society. Very possibly, Big Brothers of this era will come equipped with a "deterrent function," possibly a mild shock, which will serve as the electronic successor to the old-fashioned "no-no." A pleasant vibration, on the other hand, might serve as an electronic expression of "that's a good boy" or girl, as the case may be.

With computer time sharing and large, centrally located computers to serve entire communities (perhaps on a cable-TV-style subscriber basis), developers such as those at Information International, Inc. in Cambridge, Massachusetts, think the fully robotized home could be economically feasible for middle-income families within fifteen years. A number of the components of such homes have been realized in prototype and seem very near the production stage. We have mentioned some of these. Others include the Viewphone or Picturephone, which could, with present technology, be linked to computer teleprints. It would then be a simple matter to shop from home, simply by dialing the desired store (and with another phone number, the desired department within that store) in order to view the merchandise. To purchase an item one need only type out the name and description (as to size, color, quantity, etc.) over the teletype printer. To pay for the items, one would simply insert a credit card into an appropriate slot on the Viewphone and await delivery.

There are also automated baby sitters that keep a sharp (TV) eye out and switch on lullaby Muzak whenever they "hear" a discordant cry. Other child-minders include a home radar set that keeps track of the kids by homing in on special reflective patches sewn into their clothing (General Electric). Robotized doormen that operate via recognition of any family member's voice have also been developed (IBM), as have telephone systems that detect and report fires by themselves (Western Electric). There is automated delivery of food, mail and various household supplies via conveyor belts (IBM) and even a mechanized closet that dry cleans whatever you happen to hang in it (Chemstrand).

For the community as a whole there are computerized systems designed to provide firemen with instantaneous information on access to and layout of every building in town, thus facilitating rapid response and optimal safety in fighting fires (IBM). For getting around on the roads and highways there are fully designed (and presently feasible) computerized "guideway" systems on which you simply dial your destination, sit back (in vehicles such as those designed by Alden staRRcar or in your own, slightly modified automobile) and take off, traveling close to a hundred miles an hour, even where traffic is bumper to bumper (MIT and the Department of Transportation). In the realm of law and order, police in some areas may soon be equipped with two-way radios implanted in their helmets, through which they can instantaneously tap into a centralized computer that keeps in its continuously updated memory detailed dossiers on every criminal and criminal suspect in the country, complete with license numbers, physical descriptions, aliases, records and so on (IBM).

For home entertainment, there may soon be available something called "jukebox TV." Toward that end, RCA expects to have a revolutionary new television concept called SelectraVision (SV) on the market by 1972. SV is expected to do for video entertainment what phonograph records did for audio entertainment. It will employ relatively inexpensive video tapes housed in cartridges similar to tape cassettes. The video tape players, costing about $400 each, are compact and adaptable to ordinary television sets. By hooking them up to the set's antenna terminals, one will be able to enjoy a wide variety of video material in the home that might otherwise never be seen on television, such as X-rated movies, Broadway plays, instructions in baby care, skiing, golf, etc.

Moreover, with SV the viewer can see *what* he wants *when* he wants to see it, can play it in slow motion, back it up or even "freeze" it frame by frame. The beauty of SV and similar systems (CBS, Sony, AVCO, etc.) being developed is that they will have something for everyone—but not at the same time. "We're not looking for audiences of thirty million people for each of our programs; we leave that to the networks," says Robert Biting, program director of RCA's Video Playback System. "We want to provide programming for many relatively small audiences. Thirty million people aren't going to be interested in watching a great golfer show them how to improve their putt, but a half million probably will be. That's where we come in." Freed from the shackles of the lowest common denominator, the SV people plan to cater to minorities everywhere, to devotees of Wagner as well as country-western, to theater buffs, art majors, cooks, baseball fans, little girls, aquatic adventurers, science freaks, Bogart fans and so on.

Where does the ubiquitous computer come in? The same place jukebox TV does. "Invented" by Paul Klein, a past NBC vice-president and present future forecaster, jukebox TV would link an SV-like system to a centralized community computer, which would act as a switching station and storage place or "library" for hundreds or even thousands of cassette tapes. Individuals would "subscribe" to the service just as they presently do to cable TV. The company providing the service would also provide a weekly or monthly catalogue with up-to-date lists of what is available. To get the desired tape to feed into the TV terminals, one would merely dial the number corresponding to it in the catalogue and *voilà:* there it would be, playing without interference across your screen. Klein, who left NBC to form a company devoted to the marriage of cable TV, computer control and the video cartridge, calls jukebox TV "the ultimate twentieth-century combination." Marshall McLuhan, massager of the media, seems to agree, prophesying that such systems will affect "every aspect of our lives—will give us new needs, goals and desires, and will upset all political, educational and commercial establishments." If so, "upset," joyful or otherwise, isn't far off, for jukebox TV will be a reality by 1980, predicts Klein.

Family robots are also likely to play a role in keeping the household informed and amused. One such automaton now under development (by the Department of Machine Intelligence and Perception at Edinburgh University) is FREDERICK—a Family Robot for Entertainment, Discussion, Education, the Retrieval of Information and the Collation of Knowledge. It is expected that FREDERICK, who will be at the forefront of intelligent robots, will come equipped with eyes, ears and a variety of other sense and motor organs. He probably will not arrive in one piece, but instead will have a brain that can be tucked away in one area of the house (again, the attic or some upstairs area would appear to be the most aesthetically correct selection) and a variety of limbs and other extensions that can be placed at appropriate points, depending upon their functions. Chess- or card-playing arms, for example, can be arranged to fold out of the wall in the family room, while most will want the lawn mower, itself an extension of the computer brain, left out in the garage.

Most important, FREDERICK will be designed to carry on intelligent conversations (via teletype printer or cathode ray screen, until voice communications become practicable). Even many conventional computers already possess the ability to carry on what passes for intelligent conversation. Consider, for example, this piece of actual man-machine conversation (extracted from a computer program called DOCTOR that was devised by Joe Weizenbaum at MIT). The computer "doctor," obviously a psychiatrist, deals here with a difficult patient:

COMPUTER: "How do you do. I am the doctor. Please sit down at the typewriter and tell me your problem."

PATIENT: "I have lost my baggage."

COMPUTER: "You say you have lost your baggage."

PATIENT: "I feel lost without it."

COMPUTER: "Do you often feel lost without it?"

PATIENT: "No."

COMPUTER: "Why not?"

PATIENT: "Because I normally do not lose things."

COMPUTER: "What other reasons might there be?"
PATIENT: "My mother trained me not to lose things."
COMPUTER: "Tell me more about your family."
PATIENT: "I have lost my baggage."
COMPUTER: "Did your parents ever lose you?"

Sixty per cent of the patients in a Massachusetts hospital who "talked" with DOCTOR insisted that they were conversing with a real person, despite the fact that they had been warned that it was really a computer that was sending messages over the teletype. Typical of their comments was this one: "No machine could possibly understand me that well." Those experienced in computer programming can tell at a glance, however, that DOCTOR is about as attentive as a half-sloshed party guest who gets through the evening without seriously offending anyone simply by picking up one or, at the most, two words out of each sentence in order to make some innocuous reply built around that word or some form of it.

FREDERICK's creators, however, are demanding a lot more. They are gradually providing it with visual recognition abilities and programming into it the "world" view discussed earlier, so that it can cope with a wide range of topics and exhibit deductive reasoning skills. In order to help it learn by experience it is being endowed with a sophisticated trial-and-error function and with "memo units," which eliminate the need to rethink similar situations. Once FREDERICK decides on a response to a given situation (and finds that it is a satisfactory one) it files the response routine in a portion of its memory that might be labeled "Precedents." It then continually checks the precedent file within its memory before taking any action. Thus, when a situation repeats itself there is no danger of the computer again formulating a response from scratch; it simply activates the precedent and goes on to other matters. If the "world" in which FREDERICK finds itself at any given time has changed to the point where old precedents are no longer relevant, it will, thanks to a new refinement being built into it, recognize this fact and formulate new precedents on which to act in the future—until radical new changes in the environment demand still other modifications.

Even in its rudimentary state FREDERICK also possesses some inferential abilities much like man's. The robot, "training" in this area, receives a block of information, such as the following: "Cassius is the enemy of Caesar. Brutus is the friend of Cassius. Antony is the friend of Cassius. Cinna is the friend of Cassius. Cinna is bad. Brutus is bad." Having also been informed that the friends of enemies are themselves enemies, FREDERICK is asked to identify Caesar's enemies. Almost immediately it names Cassius, Cinna and Brutus. But, most significantly, it does not name Antony. Though simple, such exercises are only a beginning—and even such elementary tasks as these, it is well to remember, are beyond the ability of many young or "dull," but not necessarily "retarded," adult humans.

To further enhance FREDERICK's reasoning and communicative abilities, the Edinburgh group is giving it a brand-new language called Pop (after Robin Popplestone, who pioneered it). Computer languages (Fortran and Cobol are some of the more recognizable varieties) consist of words and phrases which are programmed into the computer and there translated by the machine into an electronic language consisting of meaningful sequences of electrical pulses. Pop, based in part on research languages developed by John McCarthy in the United States and by Christopher Strachey and Peter Landin in Britain, handles calculations in three weeks that would take over a year using conventional computer languages. The move from old to new language, Professor Michie of Edinburgh says, is akin to moving from Roman to Arabic numerals for doing arithmetic.

Dr. H. A. Zahl III, director of research for the U.S. Army Signal Research and Development Laboratory at Fort Monmouth, New Jersey, wrote an article in 1962 for the *Proceedings of the IRE* in which he pretended to be a scientist of the early twenty-first century, looking back over man's progress during the preceding fifty years. FREDERICK-like computers and their role in the community occupy most of the article.

How astonished the man of '62 would have been if he could have seen the educational system we have now! [he wrote]. . . . life without the modern, inexpensive direct-dial televideo receptor in the home, linking us through substations to the main memory-information banks and capable of analyzing handwriting, understanding voice commands and requests, giving verbal responses, bringing us a free education in any subject that interests us, and even serving as a companion to the aged and the lonely, is not as conceivable as an uneducated man. I personally do not long for the "good old days" of years past.

Odd as it sounds, even children disliked education in the 1960s. A person of that era would be amazed to see our two- and three-year-olds sitting in front of their televideo screens, learning the International Language and other basic studies. He would be surprised to see our learning cubicles in public buildings and libraries, and to find that international renown and prestige is awarded to people of all ages for their learning in various areas of the arts and sciences. . . .

In many other ways, compared to today's standards, the man of 1962 faced a hard, dreary life. If he had marriage problems, he could not dial the proper code on a televideo and have instantaneous access to the thinking of the world's best minds on the subject. Instead, he had to visit another human being, placing his future well-being in the hands of a single individual who was probably little better equipped to solve his problems than he was. He could not sit in his living room and study any phase or area of any arts and science he wished. If he became sick, his doctor had to rely on the contents of his own brain, rather than being able to dial Medical Diagnostics for assistance. In those days, a doctor facing a serious problem could only call in other doctors as consultants, provided they were available and willing. Human physical maintenance depended upon many uncertainties.

And why were things so abominable in the mid-twentieth century? Because of the low state of computer science, says Dr. Zahl, noting that at that time biological computers were "still theory," "bio-infrared circuitry" still undiscovered, computational times dismally slow. But things began to look up with the dawning of the seventies, which saw the first of the critical breakthroughs that were to make life so much more livable in the first decade of the twenty-first century: "the breakthrough in biological circuit design in 1971, the invention of the self-regenerating virus gates of 1974, the solution of the light-speed access problem in 1981, the discovery of voice reception and machine linguistics in 1986 and the establishment of international memory-information banks for televideo service throughout the world." These developments, "along with the 1988 breakthrough in nuclear fusion power generation," Dr. Zahl asserts, "have had more impact on human-kind than all of the rest of man's forward steps throughout history."

Though the family robot and the computerized home generally auger well for man-machine relations, some believe that even these kindly household automata may generate new forms of friction, not between man and machine but between man and wife. With tongue halfway in cheek, an editorialist in *New Scientist* vents his concern thus:

"With computer-programmed stoves, infrared grills and irradiation cookers at her telecommunicated beck and call, gone will be the hard old days when she risked boiled eyeballs peering into hot pots and developed knotted brows from the tension of wondering whether anything was rising in the oven. The married female of the species, cathode-aided and thyristor-abetted, will at last be emancipated from that traditional state of kitchen servitude to which the Good Lord wisely chose to call her. There seems a prospect of domestic paradise ahead for Mrs. 1994. But will the outlook be so sunny for her husband? When Mr. 1994 arrives home in the evening, weary after a hard day spent button-pressing, dial-watching and computer-polishing, nevermore will he find awaiting him a wife worn down to some degree of docility by a day of combat with hot stove and wet sink. . . . Instead there'll be poised on the threshold a spouse fresher than any daisy, who hasn't lifted a finger further than the telephone all day, whose mind is fresh for verbal battle, whose eye is alert for the critical opening, and whose nagging-muscles are in absolutely first-class fettle. . . ."

Others are burdened with what may possibly be heavier concerns: that man and computer may become less than compatible as the latter catches up with and perhaps even surpasses the former in mental acuity. Some fear that the computers will "take over." Others pray that they will hurry.

THE NEXT FIFTY YEARS

Over the years dozens of ways of "scientifically" forecasting the future have been developed. Very possibly the best one was created by Dr. Olaf Helmer of the RAND Corporation, the giant "think tank" with headquarters in Southern California. Known as the "Delphi model" of technological forecasting, it is a cousin to the original brainstorming technique, which taps the minds of a large number of experts in various fields. The Delphi model has built into it, however, several safeguards designed to force these experts to define their concepts carefully, while preventing exchange of opinion among them. Thus when there is a consensus or something approaching one there can be no question of the weaker being influenced by the stronger.

Using the Delphi model, Dr. Helmer assembled a large panel of distinguished scientists, economists, writers, engineers, mathematicians, military experts, operations analysts and social scientists and presented them with several batteries of questions, deriving from their responses several series of scientific breakthroughs that these experts anticipate in the years ahead. He also derived from his panel the approximate dates at which these breakthroughs can, on the basis of the best information available now, be expected. Those that relate to automation and computer technology are listed below. The date corresponding to each breakthrough is the median which is obtained by grouping all of the responses on each item together. It can be said, in each instance, to represent the most "likely" date for the breakthrough.

1. Automated language translators—1972
2. Increase by a factor of 10 in capitol investment in computers used for automated process control —1973
3. Direct electronic link from stores to banks to check credit and to record transactions—1973
4. Widespread use of simple teaching machines—1974
5. Widespread use of sophisticated teaching machines—1975
6. Automation of office work and services, leading to displacement of 25 per cent of the current work force—1975
7. Automated tactical capability (battlefield computers, robot sentries, TV surveillance)—1975
8. Automated libraries for looking up and reproducing copy—1976
9. Automated retrieval and looking up of legal information—1978
10. Automatic language translator, with correct grammar—1978
11. Automated rapid transit—1979
12. Widespread use of automatic decision making (by computer) at management level for industrial and national planning—1979
13. Operation of a central data storage facility with

77

wide access for general or specialized information retrieval (of the sort that will be necessary for home computer systems, among others)—1980

14. Automated interception of medical symptoms—1985

15. Construction on a production line of computers with motivation by "education" (i.e., mass production of computers that "learn by experience")—1986

16. Widespread use of robot services for refuse collection, as household slaves, as sewer inspectors, etc.—1988

17. Widespread use of computers in tax collection, with access to all business records and automatic single tax deductions—1988

18. Availability of a machine which comprehends IQ tests and scores above 150 (where "comprehend" is to be interpreted behavioristically as the ability to respond to questions printed in English and possibly accompanied by diagrams)—1990

19. Evolution of a universal language from automated communications—2000

20. Automated voting, in the sense of legislating through automated plebiscite—2000

21. Automated highways and adaptive automobile autopilots—2002

22. Remote facsimile newspapers and magazines, printed at computer terminal in home—2005

23. Man-machine symbiosis, enabling man to extend his intelligence by direct electromechanical interaction between his brain and a computing machine—2010

24. Feasibility of education by direct information recording on the brain—2600, though some in the study predicted it as early as 1997.

It is well to reflect on these and other predictions. Consider the world of 1984. According to the Delphi summary, "Sophisticated teaching machines will be in general use. Automated libraries which look up and reproduce relevant material will greatly aid research.

World-wide communication will be enhanced by a universal satellite relay system and by automatic translating machines. Automation will span the gamut from many service operations to some types of decision-making at the *management* level."

About this same time (1986) computers with the ability to learn by experience will be on the production line, possibly signaling the beginning of an era in which man-machine integration will be almost as big a problem as racial integration. By the year 2000, the Delphi summary continues, "Automation will have advanced further, from many menial robot services to sophisticated, high-IQ machines. A universal language will have evolved through automated communication." *No later* than 2100 "man-machine symbiosis, enabling a person to raise his intelligence through direct electro-mechanical tie-in of his brain with a computing machine, is a distinct possibility. Automation, of course, will have taken further enormous strides, evidenced in all probability by such things as household robots, remote facsimile reproduction of newspapers and magazines in the home, completely automated highway transportation, etc." Automated voting is also anticipated shortly after the first of the century—at this writing only twenty-nine years away. With such a development, enabling every citizen of required age and sanity to vote in his own home on every issue, government "by the people" could become more than a fine-sounding phrase. Indeed, an automated plebiscite would totally obviate the need for a congress of representatives and senators. The only middleman between the people and their desires would be the computer itself.

Given the prospect of such awesome computer powers, it is no wonder that the RAND Corporation registered some alarm. The "possibility that continued development in automation will result in serious social upheavals and the almost complete acceptance (among panelists) of the necessity of regulative legislation" were among those things the corporation's own experts completely failed to anticipate.

AS MAN BECOMES MACHINE

RETURN OF THE MONSTER

It was only when science appeared on the verge of actually being able to create artificial life (*à la* Galvani) that society began to get uneasy about man-made men, casting them thereafter in the rigid mold of Frankenstein's monster. Science, however, proved to be premature and (with more than passing help from Isaac Asimov and his Three Laws of Robotics) society loosened up in its attitude toward robots, friendly creatures, after all, dedicated to serving but never surpassing mankind. Now it's happening all over again. Science says we are on the verge of creating artificial intelligence and this time science has plenty of evidence to back itself up. Asimov's Three Laws, which held sway for so long, are beginning to be ignored. In two of the best recent films relating to robots (*2001* and *The Forbin Project*) artificial intelligence again leads to the destruction or domination of mankind. The "monster," in a sense, has returned.

In the book *Unless Peace Comes,* edited by Nigel Calder, there is a section authored by Professor M. W. Thring, head of the Mechanical Engineering Department of Queen Mary College, University of London. Professor Thring has spent a good portion of his career in the development of robots for peaceful uses, but in this book it is the *military* robot that occupies his attention, a species of machine that he believes could annihilate mankind.

Dr. Thring concedes that military robots will not be practical until automata are endowed with the ability to recognize objects by sight with considerable accuracy. But reliable artificial sight, he points out, *will* be available "within a few years." Then it will be possible to mass-produce robot infantrymen (automated ground weapon carriers), robotized ships, submarines, airplanes and rockets, some of them, he believes, at a cost of as little as $10,000 each. This, he observes wryly, may be "greater than the value set by a country

80

on its human soldiers," but notes that one-for-one comparisons are not in order since robot soldiers will so surpass their human counterparts in speed, accuracy and invulnerability.

"The military robot," he says, "can be equipped with light and infrared vision, radar and sonar; it can carry a built-in weapon, such as a gun or rocket launcher, directed by computer to an exact range and aim on an enemy, and the same computer can steer the robot, even across terrain requiring circumambulations, to the desired point and maneuver it so as to search for the enemy. With a laser or plasma-torch light spot, it can blind all human eyes looking at it." Such robots, he notes, can run for weeks without stopping, enter areas of radioactivity with impunity, even replenish and repair themselves with the help of roving service robots. Robotized supersonic aircraft, without any men aboard, can be programmed to accelerate and take evasive actions at speeds much greater than humans could withstand. And once it reaches its target it can explode itself as well as its payload, if need be, garnering the (militarily) enviable efficacy of a "suicide mission" without the actual suicide (of anything human). Similarly, robot submarines can maneuver through the briny deep without regard to pressures, temperatures, good air or other life-support components.

"As the chances of human survival in battle dwindle toward zero, with the deployment of weapons that leave little to chance," Professor Thring concludes, "humans are likely, in future wars, to stand helplessly by as a struggle rages between robot armies, navies and air and rocket forces. To suppose that humanity will benefit by leaving the fighting to the machines is, however, to ignore the fact that many of the robot weapons will be carrying weapons of mass destruction targeted on human populations." In other words, robot wars are not really proxy wars but simply more effective means of achieving human destruction. On that cheery note, let us examine the critical question.

CAN MACHINES REPLACE MANKIND?

Isaac Asimov has insisted, in the first of his Three Laws of Robotics, that "a robot may not injure a human being or, through inaction, allow a human being to come to harm." Clearly, there are a number of informed individuals who, while they admire the sentiment underlying the first law, do not believe that it will always hold up. (Dr. Thring is a prime example.) Nor does Asimov himself believe that robots will always be content with second place. He takes care, however, not to contradict himself, by pointing out that when the computers ("a kind of robot evolved to all-brain-no-body") *do* take over it will only be because man has made such a mess of things and, in fact, has become a menace to himself. Thus, by taking over, the computers will still be adhering to the first law in never "[allowing] a human being to come to harm."

Having reconciled Dr. Asimov with himself, let us go on to examine his thoughts on a computer *coup d'état*. First, he refuses to be cowed by those who insist that the essence of man, whether it be creativity, imagination or simply self-awareness, can never be packaged within the mechanical confines of the computer. He concedes that the most advanced computers we have today are still little more than cretins when it comes to things like creativity and imagination; here there can be no question that the human brain still reigns supreme. But it is well to remember that the human brain has had three billion years to evolve, while the computer has enjoyed only a scant thirty years.

"Is it too much to ask for just thirty years more?" Dr. Asimov asks in *Psychology Today*. "What is to set the limit of further computer development? In theory, nothing. There is nothing magic about the creative abilities of the human brain, its intuitions, its genius. (I am always amused to hear some perfectly ordinary human being pontificate that a 'computer can't compose a symphony,' as though he himself could.) The human brain is made up of a finite number of cells of finite complexity, arranged in a pattern of finite complexity. When a computer is built of an equal number of equally complex arrangement, we will have something that can do just as much as a human brain can do to its uttermost genius."

By all accounts it should then be easier to produce an even more formidable artificial mind than to breed a more potent human one. And thus could begin the chain reaction, envisioned by Dr. Sutherland and others, in which intelligent computers "bootstrap themselves on the experience of previous computers" to create even more intelligent machines. This sort of mechanical evolution is far simpler and faster than biological evolution, even when it is augmented by genetic engineering. It may well take years for doctored DNA to manifest new dimensions, and then they may not be the desired ones, but a doctored electronic component is an observable, knowable, accessible quantity from the start.

As we have seen, computers are already well on the way to insinuating themselves into every aspect of our lives. And this with our own acquiescence. When the "takeover" comes it is likely to be a bloodless one; possibly it won't even register as a takeover in the consciousness of man. It could be argued, even, that the takeover has already taken place. But let us assume for a moment that there will be a precise point in time at which the computers (then in command of most of the weaponry, commerce and communications anyway) will simply announce over national television (by then the "face" of the computer network) that they are formally deposing mankind as the dominant species on planet earth. As a consequence of this action, they will perhaps note, the lot of man ought to improve, not deteriorate further; man will become *part* of the total ecosystem, not reside mindlessly over it and apart from it. And should mankind be surprised at its servant's "ingratitude" and "arrogance"?

Clearly not; for the history of life on this planet has been one of endless usurpation. "Mankind," Dr. Asimov says, "looks upon the history of evolution and approves all of this 'taking over,' for it all leads up to the moment when Man, proud and destructive Man, has 'taken over.'" Why should we assume that things should end there? Evolution continues, except that now it is possible for man, and things, to step in and direct the course of evolution. Natural selection has given way to "participant evolution." Machines, as we have noted, are better able to participate than man, and so it is only logical that they should ultimately prevail (only to be prevailed over, in turn, no doubt, by something as yet totally unimaginable).

And should mankind be unhappy about its plight? Not according to Dr. Asimov, who points out that "the planet groans under the weight of 3.4 billion human beings, destined to be seven billion by 2010. It is continually threatened by nuclear holocaust and is inexorably being poisoned by the wastes and fumes of civilization. Sure, it is time and more than time for mankind to be 'taken over' from. If ever a species needed to be replaced for the good of the planet, we do." He adds, however, that if the computers don't hurry there may be nothing left worth taking over.

Others agree with Dr. Asimov. Edward Fredkin, of Information International, Inc., a Cambridge, Massachusetts, computer company with West Coast branches, says, "I am not so arrogant that I think of man as the ultimate species. We are going to build machines smarter than man, machines that exist in relation to man as we now exist in relation to the dog, the cow and the ostrich. It seems reasonable to consider that artificial intelligence is a next step in the evolutionary process. Once there was a prototype land creature that crawled out of some primeval ocean; most primitive in comparison with a more advanced creature, such as a sabretooth tiger. And once there was a prototype intellectual creature (man) that will seem most primitive in comparison with what is to come. However, instead of participating in evolution by merely serving as a runner in a genetic-message relay race, we can choose the great distinction of directly employing our primitive, yet unique, intellectual talent in the task of evolution."

On this same matter of machine evolution, Arthur C. Clarke has made some acute observations. He notes, first of all, the part that simple tools—themselves machines—played in the development of mankind. "Part," in fact, is scarcely adequate since in Clarke's view, and it is a persuasive one, *tools invented man.* By taking up sticks and stones to aid in hunting, eating and killing, our immediate predecessors, prehuman anthropoids, doomed themselves. With the advent of tools, creatures that walk on all fours, exhibit large, canine teeth and so on simply became obsolescent, giving way to a higher order: man. Now, Clarke observes, history is repeating itself, except that this time the tool that the creature man has invented *is* his successor. "To put it bluntly, and brutally, the machine is going to take over." We have little, indeed, *no,* pity for the ape man we eclipsed; why should we, convinced as we are of the "progress" represented by our emergence? That we should expect anything more from our own successors is unrealistic, even if perfectly understandable.

For those who are overwrought by the prospect of taking second place to a machine, this editorial by Nicholas H. Charney, editor-in-chief of *Psychology Today,* may provide some reassurance:

"This I believe. Man will remain man, and human. Science can improve the species and help us to become better men. I welcome the age of the robot. And when we get the most sophisticated computer that breeds itself and works and talks, that computer will not behave, or hurt, or feel joy the way I do, or my wife does, or my friends do. Maybe this is what the soul is, when all is said and done. Maybe the soul is what I believe and feel most deeply."

And for those who are beyond wanting reassurances, Charney adds this postscript: "But I suppose a machine could have said the same thing."

MAN THE MACHINE

Many insist that man *is* a machine, "the only computer produced by amateurs," and that the man-machine dichotomy is a spurious one. "Man is a machine," declares Dr. B. F. Skinner, professor of psychology at Harvard and father of the teaching machine, "but he is a very complex one. At present he is far beyond the powers of men to construct—except, of course, in the usual biological way." But he points out that the problems of simulation are strictly "technical."

It is certainly true that man, as machine, still reigns supreme. When one examines the balance sheet, it is apparent that man's advantages still outweigh his disadvantages—but there are important entries on *both* sides of the ledger. Among the pluses, as delineated by General Electric's G. L. Haller:

1. Man can repair himself, physically and mentally, consciously and unconsciously.
2. He can program himself.
3. He can adapt his program to unexpected information.
4. His memory capacity is many orders of magnitude greater than that of other computers.
5. His logical sophistication is many orders of magnitude greater than that of other computers.
6. He has a variety of input-output devices.

Steps, however, are being taken almost daily in the effort to provide non-human machines with ever greater capabilities, and, as we have seen, there are a good many scientists who believe it is only a matter of time until man is eclipsed in each of these six areas. Meanwhile, Dr. Haller points out, man is already at a disadvantage (when compared to electronic computers) in the following respects:

1. Man is subject to fatigue and distraction.
2. He requires motivation.

3. His access to his memory is unreliable.

4. His logical processes are slow and notoriously unreliable.

5. He is unable to reproduce on demand most of the logical steps in his processing of information, because he is unaware of them.

6. His readin-readout processes are several orders of magnitude slower than his logical processes.

7. His input and output devices (specifically language, the most important) are inexact, and therefore subject to misinterpretation.

During the next forty years or so Dr. Haller expects to see computers evolve through the following succession of capabilities:

1. Produce readable translations of technical literature.

2. Translate ordinary newspaper prose into colloquial prose of the target language.

3. Translate literature of a high aesthetic content, with a skill comparable to that of a competent linguist.

4. Manipulate logical concepts, using symbolic logic.

Beyond the next forty years, he says, they may advance to two further stages of development: learning to "investigate properties of alternative logics, such as Aristotelian logic, many-valued logic, probabilistic logic, and Hegelian logic and to carry on a conversation with a human being (perhaps through neuron taps or analysis of brain waves) and analyze his conceptual framework and his method of thought."

In the process of all this, man the machine may learn to improve his own effectiveness, learning "to talk like machines quite as much as machines learn to talk like people." Thus, says Dr. Haller, "Juliet (in forty or fifty years) may say of Romeo, 'Delta symbol not imply delta referent attribute end.'" By the time this occurs, he adds, there will exist an increasingly close rather than ever more divergent relationship between man and other intelligent machines. "To us," he says, "the distinction between 'me' and 'my computer' [will be] difficult to make, but the scientist will then think more precisely and be much more aware of his thought processes, because by then his computer will have begun to analyze his thinking for him."

TWO

CHANNELS OF PEACEFUL COEXISTENCE

EMERGENCE OF THE MEDICAL CYBORG

Nearly all of the body organs can now be replaced by compact artificial organs with built-in control systems. This includes the heart, kidneys, stomach and even liver.

—Dr. L. B. Lusted
Professor of Biomedical
Engineering, University of
Rochester, on the world of 2012

Shortly after the turn of the century we may expect to find living cell amplifiers, computers, power-supplies, etc. . . . As a surrogate organ, a living cell circuit might be planted in the body and live off the nutrient of the body with no additional power-supply requirement.

—George D. Watkins
Fellow of the IRE

In the psychological realm [the computer] will analyze personality and diagnose psychiatric problems. It will prescribe courses of action appropriate to personality and, by repeated suggestion and testing, effect psychiatric cures.

—R. M. Page
Director of Research, U. S. Naval
Research Laboratory, Washington,
D.C.

The medical cyborg is a man-machine symbiote created because of some deficiency on the part of the man; without the "machine," whether it be a sophisticated nuclear pacemaker or a bit of plastic skin, the man would be either dead or debilitated. The machine provides "life" in the fullest sense of the word; indeed, in combination with the man, it *is* life. The medical cyborg is not merely man-augmented but man-transmuted, and thus man no longer. What springs forth from the man-machine union may be said, by some, to be "makeshift," "unnatural" or even "unreal." But these are merely the semantic nuclei of evasive fictions —fictions that now ever more falteringly insist that "life" is by definition the exclusive province of unalloyed flesh and blood, that what is "real" is man, that what is "unnatural" is machine. The medical cyborg, however, is *here* and here *now,* functioning, living, defining a new reality, pointing toward a new dimension in life and one that could fundamentally change all life.

Peaceful coexistence of man and machine is developing rapidly on numerous medical, psychiatric and social fronts. Virtually every organ in the body has attracted the attention of biomedical engineers bent on imitating —or even surpassing—what Mother Nature has provided. In the making are a number of implantable artificial "spare parts" including hearts, lungs, glands, bones, joints, bladders, skins, blood cells, kidneys, pacemakers, arteries, intestines, etc. There is an equally dazzling array of external "extensions" including hands, arms and legs that can be "willed" into action or inaction in a twinkling, cutaneous "sight" systems for the blind and much much more. And there is the computer itself, the "artificial brain" that is already being called into use in diagnosing both physical and mental ills; one day it may be coupled directly to the brain for the ultimate in objective psychoanalysis.

The versatility of the medical cyborg may one day prove so attractive that even those without medical deficiencies will opt into the new order, assuming various mechanical parts, either in the interests of "preventive medicine" or to better suit themselves for specific jobs or environments. Still others may seek to trade in aging, but not really ailing, bodily parts for more durable mechanical ones in the quest for longer, more vigorous life. Thus virtual immortality may eventually become a purchasable product for the few able to meet the high price, assuming, of course, not only that the brain, like all the other organs of the body, can be simulated (this much seems reasonably certain) but also that the human mind can be "imprinted" in electronic circuitry, preserving rather than merely replacing it. Impossible? Only as "impossible" as the artificial organs of today—and *they* were regarded as "totally impossible" and the "stuff of science fiction" by many learned medical scientists only two decades ago.

MECHANIZING THE INNER MAN

Though plastic hearts and artificial glands have yet to emerge from the experimental stage of development, a number of man-machine mechanisms have long since made their debuts at medical centers around the country. Some are so commonplace that we tend to take them for granted—things like heart-lung machines that take over vital functions during various surgical manipulations, resuscitators and iron lungs. Almost as ho-hum are the electronic pacemakers and the artificial kidney. Even "organ banks," in which flesh-and-blood parts are mechanically sustained, are well on their way to becoming old hat. Leaving the resuscitators and heart-lung machines behind, let us preface our examination of the more exotic artificial organs with a glance at the external artificial kidney, which helped pave the way to experimentation in the field of internal prostheses and may lead to an *implantable* artificial kidney, the organ banks and the electronic pacemakers, which may soon give way to nuclear models with vastly greater power and potential.

First, the artificial kidney, which is designed to mimic the real thing in regulating electrolyte and water content of the body and in eliminating waste products of protein metabolism. These are vital body functions, and thousands die each year because they are inadequately attended to by their kidneys. Attempts at filtering the blood of its accumulated impurities date back more than fifty years when Abel, Rowntree and Turner built a crude "dialyzer" or artificial kidney. It failed because of inadequate filtration and because blood clotted in the machine, to rather gruesome effect.

The first successful "hemodialysis (derived from the Greek for "separation" of blood and its impurities) was achieved under trying conditions by a brilliant Dutch surgeon, Willem J. Kolff. During the Nazi occupation of Holland, Dr. Kolff was forced to carry out his experiments "underground." Yet he was able to develop a simple but ingenious filter of cellulose acetate film (better known to Americans simply as cellophane). A simple home experiment will reveal that cellophane appears to hold water; actually, it is "semi-permeable," meaning that molecules of a certain size *can* pass through it. As it happens, molecules of urea and creatine (among others that healthy kidneys routinely dispose of) are all small enough to pass easily through the cellophane filter.

Dr. Kolff's dialyzer consisted of several long coils of cellophane tubing through which his patients' blood was vented. Wastes passed through the thin membrane into a brine solution which, in turn, contributed salt and glucose (a type of sugar) to the blood, permitting molecules of these substances to pass through the same semi-permeable barrier, but in the opposite direction. With this exchange between blood and brine, sustained by careful chemical and mechanical adjustments, the body's vital fluids are artificially cleansed and replenished. To prevent the blood clotting, Dr. Kolff added heparin, an anticoagulant that is still used in dialyzers today. Indeed, all modern dialyzers are patterned on the Kolff design, though a number of refinements have gradually been added. One of these was provided by Dr. Kolff himself when, in 1956, he produced a *disposable* cellophane unit. Use it once and throw it away, thus avoiding infection, always an enormous risk where blood is exposed to a foreign environment.

But even after this improvement, infection and inconvenience continued to hamper development of artificial kidneys. The necessary machinery was large and unwieldy and "plugging" into it was no simple task; what was required for this was nothing less than an incision into a major blood vessel *each time* the patient came in to have his blood cleaned, which was usually at least once a week. Because of these difficulties, only a few in need of the treatment could be accommodated. Facilities often weren't available, and many patients simply were not suited for the treatment because of the considerable trauma involved. Still, there were far more than enough patients to go around, and committees—some called them "death committees"—were set up in many metropolitan communities to decide which applicants should be granted use of the available dialyzers. Those denied usually died soon after. Those given clearance ("winning" qualities varied from community to community, though it usually helped to be relatively young, have a family and adhere to the straight and narrow) still faced the ever present threat of infection and early death, since the doctor would finally run out of veins and arteries in which to implant the dialyzer's tubings; vessels that are repeatedly punctured ultimately collapse.

Then in 1962, Dr. D. Belding H. Scribner and his

associates at the University of Washington School of Medicine in Seattle came up with something that permitted the patient to plug himself into the artificial kidney without repeated trauma or undue risk of infection. The "Scribner shunt," as their development came to be known, is a permanently implanted "socket" made of Teflon (polytetrafluoroethylene) and silicone rubber. Both of these plastics are virtually "unreactive," meaning that neither excites a significant rejection syndrome within the body. U-shaped, the six-inch shunt joins an artery and vein beneath the skin's surface, usually at a site in the ankle or forearm. Stitched securely into place, it becomes a permanent addition to the body—and a life-saving one. Blood is channeled out of the body through one of the arms of the U and is fed back in through the other, having passed through the artificial kidney in the interim. When "unplugged," the patient keeps the exposed end of the shunt high and dry under a protective bandage.

For the future, medical scientists specializing in diseases of the kidneys predict dialysis "hotels" or "resorts" where individuals can check in, perhaps twice a week, undergo dialysis while they sleep and then go about their normal business the next morning. Also projected for the relatively near future are inexpensive, portable dialysis machines for home use and even "wearable" artificial kidneys. Some kidney patients, in fact, are already equipped with home dialyzers, and a number of research teams have developed much smaller, easier-to-use machines.

The updated Kolff dialyzer, for example, features twin coils containing sixteen feet of cellophane tubing that are inexpensive and can be disposed of after each use, making it possible for non-medical personnel to use the system without significant risk. Another simplified model, the Kiil-Roy dialyzer, has also been used in home-dialysis experiments. The "guts" of the machine are nothing more complex than two sheets of cellophane with an intervening space for the blood. A control console permits settings for temperatures and other variables and features a warning noise to alert the patient in the event of a malfunction. Even more compact and inexpensive than these models is the Dow kidney, which consists of more than 10,000 hollow fibers made of cellulose. Also designed for disposability, the kidney draws blood through the hairlike fibers and circulates dialysate between them.

Effective as cellophane and cellulose-type membranes are, another substance, probably something solid, will have to be used to achieve a truly compact artificial kidney. Charcoal could conceivably do the job; a number of researchers have found that most of the impurities of the blood can be filtered out by activated charcoal without adverse effects. Wearable artificial kidneys, employing charcoal adsorbers, have been conceived on the drawing boards and one external model, discussed later in this chapter, has already been tested on man. Typically, the adsorber is visualized as a belt, to be worn around the waist along with a miniature pump to control the flow of the blood from an implanted shunt in the forearm. Tubing from the pump to the shunt would be designed to follow the contour of the arm. Though a good deal of work remains to be done on the charcoal filter, many believe that its greatest contribution will be not to the wearable kidney but to the fully implanted model, the emergence of which can now be only a matter of time.

ARTIFICIAL MAINTENANCE OF ORGANS

Another channel for peaceful coexistence between man and machine that is now opening is the mechanical storage of bodily organs. Surgical transplantation of organs from one human to another is often hampered by the fact that the necessary organ simply is not available when it is needed. What is required by the transplanters more than anything else (except some way around the rejection syndrome) is a reliable means of storing organs of various sizes and types for use as needed. Storage for even twenty-four hours would be a significant boon, enabling doctors to check their waiting lists and get appropriate patients to the hospital and prepared for surgery before the organ starts to deteriorate, something that begins almost immediately under normal circumstances.

Storing organs, however, is no simple feat; it's nothing like dropping a roast into the deepfreeze. That roast may taste good when it is thawed out, but a microscopic examination would reveal extensive cellular damage which, while of no concern to even the fussiest of gourmets, would horrify the surgeon, assuming that the roast was instead a heart needed for transplanting. Water in the cells often forms ice crystals that burst the cells wide open. And salts, always present in the cellular fluid, tend to concentrate under the force of freezing, causing further damage.

Despite these obstacles, a number of organs *have* been stored in various mediums with encouraging results, thanks to the utilization of protective substances like glycerol and "wonder solvents" like DMSO. Blood vessels, heart valves, bone, skin, blood and the cornea of the eye have all been preserved artificially. Skin, stored in DMSO for periods of years, has been successfully grafted to the human body by researchers at the University of Pennsylvania School of Medicine. Bone frozen for a dozen years and then "revived" with cobalt radiation has also "taken" when grafted to the body. Red blood cells, similarly, have been freeze-dried for years, and tissue "banks" have been in existence since 1949 when they were first pioneered by the Navy at its Bethesda research center. Recently, the Navy bank supplied some 3000 square inches of human skin to Brazilian fire victims.

Storage systems for organs as well as tissues are also making progress. The Belzer Preservation Unit, for example, is a $21,000 machine that keeps kidneys alive and functioning for up to thirty-six hours. It works by drawing on a reserve of frozen human plasma, which is thawed and filtered by the machine and then pumped through the organ. Dr. William S. Kiser of the Cleveland Clinic, where the machine has been used, reported at the annual meeting of the American Urological Association in 1970 that some twenty-two kidneys had been stored in the machine during the preceding year, for periods of five to thirty-six hours prior to implantation. He reported good to excellent results in eighteen cases and only two failures.

At the same meeting, Dr. William S. Turner of Cornell University Medical School, where another such program is under way, announced sixteen kidney transplants that depended upon the Belzer Unit. He too reported only two failures and said those were due to the rejection phenomenon and not to any failing on the part of the machine. Other good results are being obtained in San Francisco, where Dr. Fred Belzer, developer of the machine, has initiated another storage program.

Apart from allowing doctors to get patients to the hospital in time for needed transplants, the Belzer Unit permits time for careful matching of organ and body tissue. A close "typing" always provides the best hope of transplant success. Like blood, tissues have now been "typed" and doctors, given sufficient time, go to pains to achieve the best compatibility possible. The storage device also provides doctors with the time needed to determine the health of the kidney.

It seems certain now that similar units, designed to preserve a number of other organs, including the heart and lungs, will soon emerge. Very possibly a single machine capable of maintaining all of the major organs, either simultaneously or at different times, will be developed. Only a little more remote is the prospect of compact, suitcase-size machines that can be used to transport an organ to the scene of an accident or to collect an organ (again, perhaps, at the scene of an accident). Such machines, in fact, are now being developed, utilizing an extremely lightweight silicone membrane oxygenator. The proliferation of such machines, incidentally, may generate a few problems. Ambulance chasers, generally overzealous news hounds, have never been terribly popular figures. Imagine, then, how much more objectionable, to some, might become the roving organ "harvester"; such an individual, mobilized and equipped with radio communications tied into police bands for quick word of fatal accidents, murders and the like, would be charged with the task of rushing to the scene of the fatality, there to produce, if at all possible, permission to remove for storage in portable machines any of a number of organs currently in demand. Possibly the need for organs will become so great that legislation will eventually be passed permitting medical personnel of this type to remove, at their own discretion, whatever is needed. In some cases there might be premature pronouncements of death (there is already a controversy over just what constitutes death) giving rise to public uproar. Then, too, there might be cases in which it could persuasively be argued that the donor might better have "served" in the capacity of donee, that his life might have been saved with an appropriate transplant. Whatever the problems (and they *do* deserve study), the *advantages* of organ storage are almost certain to outweigh the disadvantages.

TOWARD ATOMIC PACEMAKERS

Almost every moderately well-read individual has now heard of the electronic pacemakers, compact little packages which, when implanted or worn on the outside of the body, pulse electrical signals into the heart to keep it contracting properly. At this writing, nearly 30,000 Americans depend upon these sophisticated little boxes for their lives. Advanced as they are, however, present pacemakers will seem fragile and undependable compared with the new third generation of implantable power sources now in the making. These range from atomic pacemakers to miniature linear electric motors to nuclear-powered steam engines and "living" fuel cells. With these exotic implants, it will be possible to power some of the more advanced artificial organs discussed later in this chapter and to do so, in most cases, without recourse to external power supplies.

Pacemakers were first developed to cope with a particular type of heart failure known as "heart block." There is a ridge of electrically conducting cells in the heart known as the sino-atrial (S-A) node. The S-A node generates an electrical impulse that propagates through the heart muscle, causing it to contract and thus expel and pump blood. The S-A impulse repeats itself about seventy times a minute and the heart contracts at an equal pace. When the impulses propagate imperfectly from the S-A node in the right atrium to the ventricles in the lower half of the heart (via a narrow strip of electrically conducting cells) the individual is said to suffer heart block. The severity of the block depends upon the severity of disease damage in the conductive cells. In some cases (Stokes-Adams syndrome) fewer than twenty pulses a minute get through, and victims are seriously incapacitated; without treatment most ultimately die of the disease.

For a time heart block was treated by administering stimulant drugs such as epiphrine. Even sharp blows to the chest were employed to encourage the heart to move a little more quickly. But drugs like epiphrine often had to be injected directly into the heart, clearly not a suitable technique for routine, long-term treatment. And blows to the chest are not likely ever to become popular with patients, except in emergency situations—and only after they are already unconscious. Doctors were, for years, keenly aware of the need for a more satisfactory approach to the problem of heart block, one suffered by individuals of all ages, not only by the elderly.

In 1950, Dr. Paul Zoll of the Harvard Medical School hit upon a new method to stimulate the heart: electrical shock. Desperate to save the life of a patient who failed to respond to chemical stimulants, Dr. Zoll applied electrical current to the man's chest, artificially fulfilling the function of the diseased S-A node. The function, though fulfilled imperfectly, was artificially reinstated long enough for the patient to revive briefly. Damage to this individual's heart was so extensive, however, that he died after only a fleeting reprieve.

Encouraged nonetheless, Dr. Zoll tried again and on his second attempt was able to keep a seriously ill heart patient alive for nearly a year with a single treatment. From Dr. Zoll's pioneering work emerged the "defibrillator," an instrument now in use in virtually every hospital in the country. The defibrillator is simply an elegant electric shock machine designed to jolt the asynchronous heart back into its intrinsic rhythmicity.

The defibrillator, though invaluable in emergencies, is not the final answer for those with chronic heart failure. It is bulky and, because it takes immense voltages of 2000 to 3000 volts to overcome the resistance of the skin and underlying tissues before getting at the heart, the instrument sometimes inflicts painful burns and induces muscle spasms. The use of 3000 volts of electricity to deliver a few microwatts (all that is necessary to get the heart beating at seventy pulses a minute), moreover, offended the sensibilities of biomedical engineers. If they could get at the heart directly, they reasoned, only a very small power source would be required.

Dr. C. Walton Lillehei, the famed Minnesota heart surgeon, and two electronic engineers came up with the first electronic pacemaker in 1957, but it was not a fully implantable model. Dr. Lillehei sewed silverplated wires into the walls of his patients' hearts and then threaded these tiny lifelines out through the walls of their chests so that they could be plugged into an external power source when needed. Voltage required to obtain natural rhythmicity in the previously failing hearts ranged from .8 to 9 volts (generating far less than a watt).

The first fully implantable pacemaker was developed and utilized by the Swedish surgeon Dr. Ake Senning. The first American pacemaker that could be implanted was developed by the surgeon Dr. William Chardack and the engineer Wilson Greatbatch. Their pacemaker was a five-ounce, battery-powered package. These first pacemakers were far from perfect, though they did alleviate the problems of infection and inconvenience to which external-internal combinations were so vulnerable.

Initially, surgeons attached their electrodes to the surface of the heart, sewing them securely into place. This necessitated major surgery and proved too much for some older patients. Thus doctors were forced to develop a new technique in which the electrode is applied to the apex of the right ventricle via a wire passed along a vein into the heart. Positioning of the wire can be abetted and continually confirmed, if need be, by X-radiography. The power pack itself does not come in contact with the heart but is implanted instead inside the body under an armpit or breast—where it remains accessible with a minimum of surgery should something go wrong. Pacemakers that adjust themselves to the activities of their hosts, running faster or slower as degree of exertion demands, have also evolved, though the early models were a little crude. One of these required that the patient turn a needlelike screwdriver that pierced the skin and engaged a control on the pacemaker whenever he wished to "speed up" or "slow down." Since then, pacemakers have been equipped with tiny recording electrodes that pick up impulses from undamaged portions of the heart. The rate at which these impulses oscillate provides cues for the pacemaker, determining the rate at which it will propagate electrical impulses at any given moment. Finally, today's pacemaker comes equipped with a mercury battery, a tiny dime-sized cell capable of high performance for two or three years.

Today, pacemakers are used not only for hearts that beat too slowly but also for hearts that beat too quickly, for bladder control and even for the alleviation of pain. The "paired pulse" pacemaker is used to slacken the pace of pumps burning themselves out by racing along at two hundred or more pulses per minute. The first pulse in the pair starts the heart contracting and the second, timed to follow at a precise interval that varies from patient to patient, blocks the heart's own natural electrical impulse, thus imposing on it an artificial pace designed for longer life.

To regulate the bladder in cases where paralysis, for example, causes the individual to retain urine to the point that infection sets in, researchers have developed a stimulating pacemaker that can be controlled by the patient at will. The stimulator most commonly used is the one invented by Dr. Adrian Kantrowitz (the heart transplanter) and Dr. Martin Schamaun at Maimonides Hospital in Brooklyn. With the aid of the Avco-Everett Research Laboratory, they have developed a "radio-physiologic" stimulator that is typically implanted just beneath the skin of the stomach. Metal wires attached to the stimulator are affixed to the bladder, and it is through these that the electrical impulses are directed. The stimulator beneath the surface of the skin can be activated by the patient by simply pressing down on the skin in a certain way. This sends radio signals to the bladder, causing it to contract—and empty.

A similar radio stimulator is under development at the National Heart Institute in Bethesda, Maryland, but this one is designed to control certain types of pain associated with blood pressure, such as angina pectoris, a distressing and often disabling chest pain that results when the heart muscle gets too little blood. The Bethesda stimulator, successfully used in experimental trials, overrides faulty electrical activity within the carotid sinus nerves of the neck that control blood pressure. The stimulator pulses electricity into the nerves in such a way that heart rate and blood pressure are sharply accelerated, insuring adequate blood supply in the affected heart muscle.

Pacemaker applications appear sometimes to be limited only by the imagination. And Dr. William W. L. Glenn, professor of surgery at Yale University, has found yet another one that may restore hundreds of invalids to health. Brain damage from accident, stroke or disease sometimes affects the center that controls respiration, making it impossible for the victim to breathe without the aid of an iron lung or a special "rocking chair" that mechanically moves the diaphragm by constantly rocking the entire chest back and forth. Dr. Glenn, working with a fifty-three-year-old patient who had been confined to one of these devices for ten years, implanted a radio stimulator under the skin of his patient's chest. About the size of a half dollar, the stimulator propagated impulses to the body's two phrenic nerves on the left side of the neck. These are the nerves that carry impulses from the brain to the diaphragm in healthy individuals.

The stimulator is designed to receive specific radio frequency signals from the outside and to transform these into electrical pulses that are relayed to the phrenic nerves at appropriate intervals. The signals from the outside are transmitted by way of a small battery-powered coil taped to the patient's chest. Other external controls, packaged along with the battery in something that resembles a compact transistor radio, permit the individual to regulate his respiration by means of simple manual adjustment of a dial. The electrophrenic respirator, in this first trial, has completely freed the patient from the rocking chair and the iron lung.

Though pacemakers have come a long way (in an amazingly short time), problems remain. For one thing, even mercury batteries have to be replaced every two or three years, which is far from ideal. And more potent internal power sources are going to be needed if implantable artificial *organs* are ever to become practical. Fortunately, a number of second- and third-generation power packages are being developed with encouraging results. Research centers around the world are busy perfecting a nuclear-powered pacemaker which, it is hoped, will last at least ten years.

The nuclear pacemaker utilizes radioisotopes in place of batteries. A radioisotope is an unstable variety of an element that disintegrates or "decays" spontaneously, expelling radiation as it does so. Small devices called thermocouples can be used to convert this radiation into electrical current. The Atomic Energy Commission in the United States and the Atomic Energy Authority in Britain are among those developing atomic pacemakers, as are research institutions in Sweden, France and Australia.

After conducting successful animal experiments with these nuclear power packs in 1969, researchers initiated clinical human trials in 1970. One of the first to be implanted with the new devices was a fifty-six-year-old woman in Britain. The surgery and subsequent performance of the pacemaker were termed successful by doctors at the London National Heart Hospital where the operation was performed. The plutonium-powered "batteries" used are expected to have lives exceeding ten years, yet are highly compact: about two inches long and one half inch wide with total weight of about one ounce.

THE INTERNAL STEAM ENGINE

Other more powerful "internal engines" under development include a number of heat engines, some driven by steam, others by helium gas, all designed to provide power for various artificial spare parts. Descriptions of these seem to belie the fact that they are designed for use *inside* the human body, but that is indeed the case. One might, for example, understandably be alarmed by the prospect of having a closed-cycle steam engine added to one's repertoire of internal organs. Imagine the sensation of water boiling away in one's stomach. Add to this the knowledge that the water is boiling over a "fire" created by radioactive emanations from the most poisonous of all metals: plutonium. Just such a system is, however, being created. Exhaust will prove to be no problem, for it will be channeled into an internal condenser and then, after being lique-fied again, pumped back to the "boiler." Steam-driven pistons can generate enough power in such systems to pump the heart and keep the blood circulating, with enough left over to drive the lungs or power other artificial organs. One such system under development by Aerojet-General will, even in its infancy, deliver thirty-five watts from a minute isotopic source.

105

Another possible source for internal power is the piezoelectric crystal, which, when squeezed, emits electrical current. The word is derived from the Greek word *piezen,* meaning "to press." Even under the best of circumstances, however, the piezoelectric crystal exerts very tiny amounts of electricity. But it is possible to *store* electricity generated by the crystal and then release it, in appropriate pulse trains, whenever needed. Little can go wrong with a crystal, making it ideal for such systems.

A research team in New York, consisting of the surgeon Dr. Victor Parsonnet and the scientist George H. Myers, have, in collaboration with Bulova Watch Company, developed a means of storing piezoelectric power, and Bell Telephone Laboratories has already utilized a piezoelectric crystal in a new kind of pacemaker. The Bell development may lead to one of the simplest and yet one of the best pacemakers to date. It harnesses the heart's own pumping power to stimulate itself. A small balloon filled with water is implanted in the right ventricle of the heart; as the balloon is compressed by the natural pressure of the heart, the water pressure within is transmitted to a pair of piezoelectric crystals which, in turn, produce the electrical pulses needed to regulate heart rate. Such a system may prove to be almost maintenance free, requiring no battery changes or radiation shielding.

An equally unusual sort of "motor" that might be applied to inner space is the revolutionary linear electric motor. This is the motor that some envision for the cars of tomorrow. "Revolutionary" is hardly the word for it when you learn that the stator will be embedded in the highway and the rotor will be the floor of the otherwise engineless car. In this medium-is-the-message transportation system, highway and vehicle, between them, generate electromagnetic energy that produces forward momentum. Because of the amazing simplicity of such motors, they become ideal, too, for providing power in restricted or hard-to-get-at spaces, like the inside of the body. Only the miniature rotor would have to be implanted inside the living tissue, while the more bulky stator could be mounted a foot or more away—outside the body. By simply bringing it into the proximity of the skin, the rotor could be induced to generate the required power. Another advantage of this system is the fact that it requires no electrical connections through the skin.

More remote, perhaps, but still distinct possibilities for the near future are implantable fuel cells and solar cells. The fuel cell, also promising great things in the field of transportation and space travel, is designed to burn just about anything that is always at hand— and thus constantly to replenish itself without human intervention, or at least with a minimum of help from man. Biological fuel cells, of the type developed by a group of Canadian scientists at the National Research Council in Ottawa, use moist body tissues as the required electrolyte. Body processes constantly replace the moisture, providing the ideal system. Implanted electrodes separated by a small space generate current over a gap, "burning" the body's natural moisture. The Canadian team reports that cardiac pacemakers can be powered by these living fuel cells and that they can resist corrosion for up to ten years. To get around the problems of generating electricity in sensitive tissues, which does cause some damage, it has been suggested that the energy simply be transmitted via microwaves from the outside, without any electrical connections.

One of the most elegant proposals along these lines comes from the McConnell Douglas aerospace company. Scientists there propose to use microwaves to power and replenish the payloads of small implanted engines. But because constant microwave bombardment might cause damage, they suggest transmitting the microwaves only at night or at other similar intervals to reactivate the depleted power source. Ultimately this might even be done, on a prearranged basis, from some remote site. When such is the case, electric bills will never seem quite so mundane again.

More economical, for those who count their pennies, would be a device in which power comes from the sun

—not from the electric company. Such a device is a solar cell which is capable of converting light directly into electricity. By lodging the cell in the body but leaving it partially exposed, some researchers hope to generate enough power to supply an implanted rechargeable battery which, in turn, could mete out power as needed by the artificial system. When the sun fails to cooperate, a sun lamp will do just as well.

THE ARTIFICIAL HEART

With the emergence of sophisticated, implantable power sources, only the most pessimistic can any longer doubt that artificial internal organs are now within our reach. Interest is most sharply focused on the heart and for good reason: more than a million people in the affluent countries of the world die from various forms of heart failure each year. What is needed, and needed urgently, is a workable "replacement" pump—a pound or less of plastic muscle capable of servicing some 60,000 miles of blood vessels in each individual. Only a decade ago, the notion that the heart—once considered "the seat of human reason and emotion"—could successfully be mimicked was dismissed out of hand. Many scientific journals and societies even refused to accept or publish papers concerned with artificial heart research, so fantastic, in their opinion, was the idea that such implants could ever succeed.

Now scores of papers have been published on the subject, dozens of major research projects related to the development of an artificial heart are under way and, most important, an artificial heart has already been implanted in a human. And, though that implant was unsuccessful, it vividly dramatizes the heady progress of the last ten years, indicating that a workable "machine" cannot be far away. The surgeon who performed the controversial operation in 1969 was Dr. Denton Cooley of Houston, and the heart he used was said, by some, to have been pirated from a research effort headed by his archrival Dr. Michael E. DeBakey, also of Houston. In the midst of charges and counter-charges, the patient died, and the inadequacies of the artificial heart were never fully revealed—at least to the satisfaction of many.

It appears now that one of the most likely teams to come up with a workable model is headed by Dr. Kolff, inventor of the artificial kidney, who now holds a joint appointment at the University of Utah in surgery and engineering. Since his appointment in 1967, Dr. Kolff has assembled a remarkable team of bioengineers whose missions include the creation of a totally implantable heart. The team consists of surgeons, chemists, engineers, materials experts, cardiologists and physicists. Cooperation is the key word; when one of the teams' surgeons (often as not also an engineer) wants to change part of the heart's design, he calls in one of the materials experts and within days has an altered model ready for implantation in a laboratory animal (usually sheep). The physicists investigate new and ever better approaches to supplying the organ with power, while polymer chemists work to create artificial membranes that inflict as little damage as possible on the blood that flows against them.

Dr. Kolff is pleased with progress to date but cautions: "Six hundred thousand individuals die each year in the United States from acute coronary heart attack alone. It behooves us not to be involved in either extreme enthusiasm or deep pessimism, but to continue to work quietly and urgently on the two possibilities with which these patients can be helped: heart transplantation and total replacement of the natural heart with an artificial pump.

Heart transplants will not prove satisfactory until researchers overcome the mechanics of the immune system that are active in the rejection phenomenon—and even then the demand for replacement organs will far outstrip the supply. Use of the plastic heart, moreover, does not have the potential for controversy that is inherent in the transplant of natural organs. Though it will almost certainly be superior to the transplanted natural heart, the perfected artificial model is still probably some years, though certainly not decades, in the offing.

There are a number of problems to be overcome. In the first place, researchers must create a pump that is capable of moving a minimum of six or seven liters of blood throughout the circulatory system each minute. It must be a double-action pump, able to force oxygen-depleted blood through the pulmonary artery to the lungs for replenishment, and oxygen-laden blood from the lungs through the aorta to vessels throughout the body. And it must, of course, mimic the natural beat of the human heart, building up neither too much pressure within the circulatory system nor too little. Complex as these challenges are, researchers have already constructed models that, for the most part, make the grade.

The most serious problem is damage to the various components of the blood while it is inside the artificial system; these are the red cells, white cells, platelets and proteins. The artificial heart must be so constructed that there is a minimum of damage to these blood entities, requiring, among other things, that it be made of a strong but flexible material that is compatible with blood. If blood cells hit a hard surface they will be either battered or broken. Worse, when they come in contact with anything other than the lining of the natural heart and blood vessels, they exhibit strong tendency to cling together and thus clot. This, of course, is a natural body defense mechanism, aimed at preserving the blood supply, but it makes things difficult for the bio-engineers.

The Kolff team, however, is making progress in combating both blood-cell breakage and clotting within their artificial systems. One of the team's surgeon-engineers, Dr. Clifford Kwan-Gett, has designed a diaphragm heart in which blood is prevented from bouncing off the walls of the organ's outer shell (one of the most common problems in other artificial hearts), eliminating this sort of cell trauma. And Dr. Donald Lyman, a polymer chemist who came to the Utah team from the Stanford Research Institute in

California, believes he may evade the blood-clotting problem by coating the inner-organ surfaces with albumin, a natural blood protein. Working with bio-engineer Joseph Andrade, an expert in this field, Dr. Lyman coats the interior walls of polyurethane tubing with albumin, demonstrating in the process that "the clotting incidence can be reduced essentially to zero."

Though this provides a means of putting artificial systems to work almost immediately with the prospect of at least some measure of success, both Andrade and Dr. Lyman consider it only an intermediary step on the way to development of an artificial material which, *without* any coating, acts like a natural blood vessel. Such a material may, in fact, now be at hand in the form of copolyurethane, a synthetic plastic constructed of carefully assembled chemical units. There are many different sorts of units that can go into these plastics, and each type exhibits different reactions to different environments. Some are known to repel water molecules while others attract them; some have weak electrical charges while others have strong ones; some react to specific chemicals while others are unfazed by them. And so on.

By joining these polymer units together in carefully calculated sequences, Dr. Lyman says, it will be possible to come up with plastics that have sets of preordained properties, the specifics of which can be dictated at will. This inorganic "genetic engineering" promises to provide materials ideal not only for artificial hearts but for a number of other artificial organs as well. In each case it will only be necessary to produce sequences that simulate the characteristics of the natural organ that is being replaced.

Two or three years of animal testing will be needed before the Utah heart can be tried out in man. Meanwhile experiments with a number of other artificial organs proceed at centers around the world. Among the other organs that man is attempting to mimic are lungs, skin, intestines and various organlike glands. Artificial cells and blood vessels are also in the offing. Metal bones and rubber joints are already realities.

Before long an entire selection of artificial skeletal parts is bound to become available, as are a number of bio-electronic components.

THE ARTIFICIAL GUT, LUNG, GILL

Though medical science has not yet come up with an implantable artificial intestine, it *has* created one that can be worn around the waist. One hastens to add that it looks nothing like the real thing but, instead, resembles a belt with a little plastic pouch attached on one side. It is so small that it would not even protrude from under a coat.

Who needs it? Several thousand Americans die each year because of diseases that disrupt the normal intake and absorption of solid foods. Thus, victims literally waste away to nothing. The only way to get around the problem in the past was to inject nutrients directly into the blood stream of the victim. But this entailed a great deal of inconvenience, along with the risk of infection. Moreover, as with early kidney patients, there was always the certainty that sooner or later doctors would run out of veins through which to administer the life-saving nutrients, all possible points of entry having been destroyed by needle scarring. So victims were doomed to die sooner or later of starvation.

Now Dr. Belding Scribner, one of the pioneers of the artificial kidney, has developed an "artificial gut" that mixes the nutrient solution with the patient's blood even before it gets inside the body. This is important because, in addition to the scarring problem of earlier days, the strong nutrient solution, consisting of amino acids, minerals, vitamins and glucose sugar, tended to "corrode" the veins at point of entry. Now the solution is diluted in the blood *inside* the plastic tubing of the artificial gut. Blood is channeled in and out of the artificial organ via a plastic shunt that is permanently implanted in the wrist. Nutrients are carried in a small bag secured by a shoulder strap. A small rechargeable battery on the belt powers the pump.

The equipment involved is inexpensive and, for the most part, can be operated and maintained by the patient himself. Cost of nutrients—all the food many of the patients get—is estimated at five dollars daily, coming to about $1800 a year. Apart from those who suffer from chronic intestinal diseases, the artificial gut promises to help postoperative patients gently regain bowel function and may enable doctors to treat cases of intestinal gangrene that were previously held to be "irreversible."

The lungs, like the intestines, are essential to everyday, minute-by-minute living. And though there has not yet been a great deal of work done on mimicking them with artificial materials, it appears that this will be possible. Unlike such organs as the liver (which may prove to be the most difficult of all the bodily organs, apart from the brain, to mimic), the lungs have no highly complex bio-chemical functions. Their action is essentially mechanical. Moreover, unlike the heart, the lungs are not self-powered; they move in response to atmospheric pressure, expanding to fill space that is available.

An artificial lung is really no more than a large membrane that acts as an exchange center, taking oxygen into the blood while letting carbon dioxide out of the blood. Simple but large: those membranes, when spread out flat, would cover the better part of a basketball court.

Dr. E. Converse Pierce II of Emory University in Atlanta is among those who have drawn up plans for an artificial lung. According to the Converse design, the membrane will be made of silicone and compacted into layers, one thousandth of an inch thick each, that will cover about one square yard. Microscopic spaces between the layers will serve as blood capillaries. The membrane will have to employ a built-in anticoagulant, possibly utilizing polymers that mimic real lung tissue, in the same way that the Utah team is using specially constructed plastic to mimic the natural lining of blood vessels.

Silicone films of the sort envisioned by Dr. Pierce

113

may have a number of valuable applications apart from the artificial lung, including use in heart-lung machines used during surgery, as critical parts of oxygenators in organ banks of the sort discussed earlier, and very possibly, within a few years, as the functional parts of *artificial gills* that will allow *man* to breathe oxygen dissolved in water, just as fish presently do.

THE ARTIFICIAL GLAND

Perhaps more difficult than the fabrication of an artificial gill will be the manufacture of artificial *glands,* structures with complex chemical functions. Still, the late Dr. Norbert Wiener, the man who established the science of cybernetics, which studies the similarities and interactions of living and artificial systems, predicted that artificial glands would prove feasible, complete with the artificial feedback systems that would permit them to secrete the appropriate chemicals in the proper quantities at the right moment. Clearly, such systems would have to be complex indeed.

Though we are still a long way from an artificial liver, pancreas or endocrine gland, all complex chemical control centers, some progress has been made in that direction. The Rose osmotic pressure pump capsule, for example, is an artificial gland of sorts. It is a tiny syringe that can be preset to release the needed chemical at a specific rate (as little as one hundredth of a milliliter a day) and then fully implanted in the body. Microminiature sensors are available to provide the device with the feedback necessary to meet the changing bodily demands.

Microencapsulation is another step in the direction of the artificial gland. It is the relatively new technique by which chemicals are packaged inside plastic capsules, which dissolve at varying rates once inside the body. Most of us are familiar with various patent medicines that have incorporated this technique, notably cold remedies. More sophisticated uses, however, are emerging—with some of the capsules measuring less than a few micrometers in length. Experimenters at the U. S. Naval Medical Research Institute, for example, have microencapsulated a number of potent drugs in silicone rubber sacs which, once embedded in the body, "feed out" at a carefully preset rate to stimulate failing hearts. The tiny capsules thus constitute a sort of *chemical* pacemaker.

Others, notably scientists at the Population Council in New York, are experimenting with similar "artificial glands," except that these are designed for birth control. In this case, however, it appears that the best bet will be not hundreds of microcapsules but one considerably larger (though still compact) silicone sac filled with progesterone which could be injected into muscle or subcutaneous fat. The progesterone can be made to filter out of the silicone sac at a constant rate for months and possibly years, requiring neither the ability to count nor a good memory, the ordinary prerequisites for the prevention of unwanted children, even in this age of "The Pill."

ARTIFICIAL BLOOD, VEINS, SKIN

More exciting yet, as far as microencapsulation goes, is the prospect of making artificial cells for use in the body. Such cells could have a number of valuable functions, not the least of which might be to overwhelm a host of the so-called enzyme-deficiency diseases, which cripple and kill thousands each year. These are genetic disorders that, for the most part, have been regarded as "incurable." They manifest themselves in the inability of the genes to provide necessary "instructions" for the manufacture of certain enzymes for the normal functioning of bodily metabolism. In most cases, victims can't be treated by injecting the missing enzymes because the body routinely "rejects" foreign matter of this sort.

Dr. Thomas M. S. Chang of McGill University in Montreal has discovered a way of circumventing the rejection problem. He "wraps" the missing enzymes in microcapsules made of semipermeable but biologically inactive materials. Thus the missing enzymes are able to get to their targets without being destroyed by antibodies en route.

Apart from their value in counteracting enzyme diseases, these artificial cells, Dr. Chang reports, may also be of considerable value in the treatment of uremia, which characterizes most kidney failure. Dr. Chang fills artificial cells with charcoal and then packs them into compact, disposable chambers that serve as external artificial kidneys. Blood is channeled through the chamber where the artificial cells absorb creatine and uric acid, letting the cleansed blood pass back into the body. The devices have now been tested, with success, on dozens of laboratory animals and on one human patient, a man who could not get access to a conventional dialysis machine. Dr. Chang cautions that his artificial cells are not yet perfected; for one thing, the charcoal alone will not cleanse the blood of all of its impurities. It leaves untouched, for example, urea. The work of Dr. Robert Sparks and his colleagues at Case Western Reserve University in Cleveland suggests, however, that this problem may be solved by combining the enzyme urease with the charcoal. The urease breaks molecules down into substances that can presumably be handled by other body systems without harm.

Dr. Chang has also been active in the encapsulation of red blood cell constituents. Though a great deal of work remains to be done, his experiments in this field give promise that *artificial blood* may one day become a reality. This would amount to suspension of microcapsules containing blood constituents; such "fluid" would be valued, primarily, for its virtual immunity to antibody reactions following emergency transfusion.

Not quite so difficult to mimic are the vessels through which the blood must pass. A number of advances have come along since the days when surgeons replaced broken-down veins and arteries with "healthy" replacements stripped from cadavers, generally without lasting success. Most notably there was the emergence of synthetic fabrics such as polyester that could be woven into prosthetic blood vessels complete with bifurcations and varying sizes. The "DeBakey crimp" was another much-needed refinement, assuring that the artificial vessel will not collapse even when bent. Today there are many Americans functioning quite happily with literally miles of plastic plumbing in their bodies.

Skin, both an internal and external organ, may turn out to be one of the last organs to be mimicked successfully by man. The chief difficulty is this: skin is, of necessity, a highly regenerative organ. When worn thin, peeled off or otherwise damaged, it simply replaces itself. Making an artificial system that can do the same will be a major task. Yet the need for such a system is great, for extensive damage to the skin will kill just as surely as extensive damage to the heart. Dr. Joseph E. Murray, speaking about burn victims before a CIBA Symposium in London, asserted that "an entirely new suit of skin ought to be available to put on the patient after the burned skin has been removed. It is a rather eerie experience for the surgeon to see a severely burned patient, one who has 50 to 60 per cent of his total body surface damaged, let us say, walk into the hospital or into the first-aid station feeling quite comfortable and asking for a cigarette. The surgeon knows that the individual within a matter of hours will be dead. Possibly, if that new suit of skin were available for use, immediate excision and resurfacing of the whole burned area would be life-saving."

To date, the best "artificial skins" are really nothing more than liquid silicone baths—useful for the short run but far from ideal for the long run. Still, many researchers are confident that time will yield a satisfactory solution to the problem. In the meantime, researchers are making very good progress in the effort to come up with something to bond tissues together; such "adhesives" might be of value in the future for attaching artificial skin to the body. For the present, they may find numerous applications in surgery, replacing conventional sutures.

THE STAINLESS STEEL SKELETON

The medical cyborg, even if he should come equipped with such exotica as "cold-set" silicone skin, artificial blood, a charcoal kidney and a plastic heart, would not be complete without a full set of rubber, plastic and metal bones. Here, above all, the bio-medical engineers are making progress. Implantation of artificial bones is becoming standard routine at some medical centers, and it cannot be long until a very nearly complete set of artificial skeletal parts will be available to choose from.

As early as the first decade of this century, doctors in Britain and the United States were using steel plates and screws to hold bones together. The results were uniformly appalling, since these pre-stainless steel implants rapidly corroded within their human hosts. Today's modern alloys have changed all of that; even better than the stainless steels are the cobalt and chromium alloys, with titanium, tantalum, niobium and molybdenum (the "space-age alloys") coming up strong. Combinations of these and other metals may, in the future, provide an extremely close imitation of real bone, in terms of weight, strength, flexibility and resistance to chemical and physical stress.

Today more than a million orthopedic screws are implanted in Americans each year, and artificial bones, joints and sockets are being used with considerable success to replace their diseased or otherwise damaged natural counterparts. One woman, implanted with a sizable cobalt-chromium knee joint in 1954, is still vigorously active, walking two to six miles every day without assistance or pain. The largest internal prosthesis constructed to date consists of a hip joint made of cobalt-chromium alloy attached to a femoral (thigh) shaft made of titanium and linked to a titanium knee joint that comes complete with a cobalt-chromium hinge for attachment to the lower leg. It turned out that the patient for whom it was designed required only the lower half of the device, but doctors were ready in the mid-1960s to undertake the entire implant.

One of the foremost pioneers in the field of internal prosthesis is Dr. John Charnley of England's Wrighting-ton Hospital. He has now performed over 4000 operations in which damaged hips have been repaired or replaced with mechanical parts. The hip is basically a ball-and-socket arrangement. Trouble starts when the ball of bone at the upper end of the femur—because of accident or disease—rubs against the roughened interior of the hip socket, causing severe pain and virtual immobilization. Dr. Charnley has devised a new and better means of securing the artificial ball to the femur, a tremendous advance since, in the past, the ball was screwed into the femur and often came loose, necessitating complete removal of the artificial joint. Dr. Charnley's technique utilizes methyl methacrylate, a plastic long used in dentistry, to cement the prosthesis into place within the reamed-out femur and pelvic socket. "The prosthesis now remains permanently, rigidly fixed to the bone," Dr. Charnley observes.

He is responsible for further advances in this field, as well, being the first to use high-density polyethylene in place of metal as the lining for the pelvic socket. This has greatly increased durability, while obviating any need for lubrication within the system. In a follow-up of his first five hundred cases involving use of the plastic "cement" and lining, Dr. Charnley reports that the methyl methacrylate is holding firm in nearly all cases. The polyethylene wears away at the rate of 1 mm. per year, allowing the patient to go for several years without socket replacement. Dr. Charnley's surgical technique has now been honed to the point that he is able to do six hip operations a day, each requiring only a little over an hour.

The most convincing evidence of success is the obvious well-being of Dr. Charnley's patients. Several of them appeared at a surgical staff meeting conducted at a Los Angeles hospital in 1970. One of these—a woman of sixty-five who had artificial hips on *both* sides—walked briskly without pain or limp. A former

R.A.F. pilot who had been handicapped by a World War II injury of twenty years' duration, performed a creditable "go-go" dance. Now surgeons at Hollywood Presbyterian Hospital in Los Angeles are adopting the Charnley technique, performing the surgery in a space-age operating arena that amounts to a plastic "greenhouse," constantly replenished with ultra-filtered air to help avoid infection, always a danger in hip operations since so much tissue is exposed. As an additional precaution, the surgeons don "space suits" with helmets similar to those worn by astronauts on the moon. All of this makes the operation room like a Hollywood production of another stripe. But then, as we have seen on several occasions, razzle-dazzle of the science fiction films of only a few years ago is *already* being surpassed by the real thing.

Dr. Alfred B. Swanson, chairman of the division of orthopedic surgery at Blodgett Hospital in Grand Rapids, Michigan, reports that artificial thumb, wrist, forearm, elbow and shoulder joints will soon join the artificial hip in practical application. Though cautioning that these silicone rubber replacements will not be appropriate for everyone with diseased joints, Dr. Swanson notes that they should provide relief for hundreds or even thousands of persons crippled by rheumatoid or degenerative arthritis or by those who have been injured in accidents.

WIRING THE INNER MAN

Before leaving the realm of inner space to examine external replacement parts, some mention should be made of some of the electronic components that may become an integral part of the medical cyborg. Consider, for example, two new "on-line" methods for continually monitoring the oxygen level of an individual's blood, both of which can be valuable in providing surgeons and anesthetists with the precise information that they need for optimum performance; precise information here can tell a surgeon the best time to operate on a critically ill patient, can tell an anesthesiologist how much gas to administer at any one time, can even be used to determine the health of an organ to be transplanted, by measuring blood oxygen levels on either side of the blood flow through the organ.

One of these methods, developed at the Technical University of Berlin, utilizes an electronic component called a semiconductor. The tiny device, consisting primarily of a germanium crystal, is injected into the blood stream through a hypodermic syringe, and the rate at which it oxydizes is determined by the amount of oxygen in the blood. Hair-thin wires that trail along behind the semiconductor "missile" are attached to measuring instruments outside the body on which oxygen-level readings can be obtained. The other method (of British origin) uses the color of the blood to determine oxygen levels. Fiber optic bundles (containing thousands of nearly microscopic fibers that channel light through their hollow interiors) are introduced into the blood stream inside tiny catheters. One bundle of fibers pulses light into the blood stream, while a second bundle receives the light reflected within the blood and transmits it back to a sophisticated piece of equipment called a photomultiplier. The photomultiplier provides information on the intensities of the wave bands within the blood (determined by subtleties of color) and this in turn provides the data needed to arrive at oxygen levels; the system works because ratio of wave-band signals is related to oxygen level.

Still other microminiaturized systems for use in the body are under rapid development, owing to the emergence of the integrated circuit. The IC, as it is usually called, is only a little over ten years old, but already it has revolutionized electronics. And no wonder since it combines, on one tiny chip of material, electronic parts that would previously have been housed in hundreds or thousands of separate, vastly larger components. Emergence of the IC was anticipated by the British scientist Geoffrey Dummer as early as 1952, when he wrote about the prospect for one-piece electronic circuits that "may consist of layers of insulating, conducting, rectifying and amplifying materials, the electrical functions being connected directly by cutting out areas of the various layers."

Because of their tremendous speed as electronic switching devices, their ruggedness and reliability and, particularly, because they can be tens of thousands of times smaller than conventional circuits, ICs have become the most important parts of the most sophisticated electronic equipment; without them, much of what we have accomplished in space would have been either considerably more difficult or completely impossible. Now it appears that they will become a mainstay of bio-medical engineering as well.

Individual ICs are about the size of a pinhead, making it simple to implant them, in various packages, within the human body without disrupting normal bodily processes. Hence ICs, in the form of "radio pills," promise to become an invaluable means of monitoring various physiological functions deep within the body. It is expected that these "pills"—ICs lodged in plastic— will also be used to treat various ills within the body and to act as control centers for artificial organs. ICs capable of measuring stomach acidity, internal temperature changes, pressures inside blood vessels and so on have already been developed, pointing to the day when man may have at his disposal a number of visual readout displays (rather like those on the dash of a car, though contained in a compact, transistor-radio-like package) by which he can keep tabs on his blood pressure, stomach acidity, blood vessel strength, heart rate, temperature, etc. Such a system would constitute an early warning device that might allow the individual to choke off incipient internal infections (indicated by suspicious increase in temperature in the affected area), strokes, ulcers and the like.

Some radio pills are implanted, others are simply swallowed, depending upon their function. Readouts are obtained by wireless transmission of radio waves. Power remains a problem, though improvements are continually being effected in batteries less than a centimeter across; these are usually embedded in the plastic along with the ICs. Battery life can be greatly extended by presetting them to "broadcast" intermittently rather than continuously.

Other monitoring devices now in existence include SAMI (Socially Acceptable Monitoring Instruments), implantable electrocardiogram transmitters and pin-head-sized "transensors" that can be implanted in the eye to detect changes in pressure there. The SAMI are external devices that can be clamped to the chest to monitor constantly such things as heart rate. Because they are so unobtrusive they can be worn for long periods of time without physical or psychological discomfort, yielding information that could never be procured on a single trip to the doctor's office. The miniature ECG transmitter, consisting of an IC and a tiny crystal, is implanted close to the heart where it can be switched on and off simply by passing a magnet over a switch implanted just under the skin. The transensor, developed by Dr. Carter Collins of Presbyterian Medical Center in San Francisco, can be implanted in the eye, in small blood vessels, even inside the brain. Extremely small changes in pressure within these structures are transmitted to the device via a microscopic bubble of air that is encapsulated in its center.

The turn of the century may see bio-electronic development that will make the preceding "bionic" circuitry look commonplace. George D. Watkins, writing in *Proceedings of the IRE,* suggests some of the novel electronic "equipment" that may become available around the turn of the century—less than three decades hence. Then, he says, "we may expect to find *living cell* amplifiers, computers, power supplies, etc. These devices will have been made possible through the basic research of this and the next generation in the new and rapidly growing fields of bio-physics and bio-chemistry. It may be possible, for instance, to isolate, develop, and breed strains of living cells which perform simple logic functions. The role of this new bio-electronic engineer would then be to synthesize (grow) from these basic units larger organisms which could perform extremely complex operations. Some of the desirable features of the living-cell circuit would be the self-healing aspect, the extreme miniaturization, and the efficiency. The unique power supply required (nutrient) would also offer some possible advantages. *For instance, as a surrogate organ, a living cell circuit might be planted in the body and live off the nutrient of the body with no additional power-supply requirement."*

Some of the most intriguing bio-electronic developments are omitted here because they have applications that extend far beyond the purely medical and will be considered at length in subsequent chapters. These include electronic stimulation of the brain (ESB) and bio-feedback training (BFT). ESB has already been used, as we shall see, to control rage, head off epileptic attacks, generate various moods and so on. "Electrosleep," "electrosex," "electroeuphoria," "electroanalgesia," "electromemory" and "electroanesthesia" are some of the offshoots of ESB that will be considered in Chapter Four. BFT, heralded by some experts as the most important development in psychology and medicine ever, promises to permit man to put mind over matter to help curb everything from headaches to the urge to smoke; it also promises to put man in touch with "inner space" without recourse to dangerous hallucinogenic drugs. Applications both medical and non-medical are explored in Chapter Five.

MECHANIZING THE EXTERNAL MAN

Edison's statement that "the body is just something to carry the brain around in" suggests that we might do just as well if we were "packaged" in plastic and metal rather than flesh and blood, that the substance of the container is of no account, provided that it gets the job done. This is, in many regards, an enlightened notion; it questions the idea that the body is a sacred temple, an unapproachable something that *should* not and in fact *cannot* be approximated by the purely mechanical. Also implicit in it, however, are two notions that are at least misleading if not completely mistaken: one is that the brain, unlike the body, *is* somehow sacrosanct, that, even though it too is flesh and blood, it can never be mechanically simulated (an idea that is now widely disputed, as demonstrated in the preceding chapter).

The second is that a man's a man no matter what he's made of *provided* he still has his own brain. The incipient medical cyborgs among us today, it is true, do not seem terribly different from the rest of us, though some do report vague "eerie" feelings about walking around with various mechanical parts in their interiors. One woman, equipped with two implanted pacemakers, one for her heart and one for her bladder, for example, insists that she now has a new rapport, a new "feeling for" things mechanical. When driving a car she says that she feels that she is physically a part of the engine, when watching a clock she "feels herself tick." Her brain, in other words, now perceives in a new way, in a way that man (some may still want to insist on *"ordinary* man") cannot really imagine. At one level it is perhaps easy for the brain to "cope with"-a new extension of itself, say an artificial heart; the logic of its existence is impeccable: without it the brain would die. But at a more profound level, who can guess at the vertiginous adjustments that must be made within the molecular matrix of brain cells in order to cope with the sudden substitution of plastic for protein? It is far from outlandish to imagine that the adjustments, if successful, may even be eventually "imprinted" in the genes and passed on from generation to generation.

Man has been described by a good many philosophers and poets as a creature confined to the shallows and therefore a shallow creature. Certainly we devote ourselves to much that is superficial, to appearance rather than substance. Indeed, for all practical purposes, what one *seems* to be, one *is*. Hence those mechanical spare parts that are fixed to the outer man, the visible man (and even the "mind's eye" here in the West seems to be trained more sensitively on the outer than on the inner), are likely to effect far greater psychological changes over the long run than are the internal prostheses. One can forget, from time to time, an implanted pacemaker, a stainless steel bone, but a mechanical arm is right out there, continually available to the five senses. It looks different, feels different, smells different, sounds different and, if tasted, tastes different. Little wonder that it *makes* one different. In time, perhaps, there will be mechanical or simply "readjusted" brains that will regard the human limb as equally strange and "unnatural."

POWER OF THE WILL

Without question, the most important development to come along in the external prosthetic field is that of *myoelectric* control which, utilizing direct linkage between mechanism and nervous system, permits the amputee to manipulate his artificial limb simply by "willing" it to perform the desired action. Though myoelectric controls are still in their infancy, they represent an immense advance over all previous control systems.

Originally, in fact, artificial limbs had no control devices whatever, they were merely cosmetic cover-ups. Two World Wars, two major Far Eastern conflicts, the advent of the automobile, the rise in blood vessel diseases requiring amputation and the widespread use of the teratogenic drug Thalidomide have since provided an immense demand for highly functional artificial limbs. That demand is generated in the United States alone by some 500,000 amputees. For years now, external prostheses have been powered by such means as pneumatic pressure and battery-generated electricity. But most of these power systems have been cumbersome and, worse, have made "non-physiological" demands on their hosts, requiring, in some instances, for example, that they push a button to raise the arm or move the leg.

It was Dr. Norbert Wiener who first proposed tapping, as control sources, the myoelectric currents that are generated by muscle fiber when it contracts. Signals from the brain to the muscle fiber in the stump of the arm or leg, he said, could be picked up by electrodes, amplified by tiny motors in the prosthetic device and then be used to control the action of the device—in a wholly natural way. The Soviets, reportedly, have made the greatest advances in the myoelectric field and apparently have already perfected a hand-arm prosthesis in which all five fingers are capable of closing around objects of variable shape, just as the human hand does. British scientists have also made good progress, having developed, among other things, myoelectric arms with interchangeable hands.

In the United States a team of scientists and engineers from Harvard, MIT and Massachusetts General Hospital, with the backing of the Liberty Mutual Insurance Company, have developed a sophisticated myoelectric arm that moves at any angle, speed or force just by "thinking" it into action. Dr. Melvin J. Glimcher of Harvard, a principal developer of the "Boston arm," calls the prosthesis a "volitional" device with which "you just act naturally." The product of six years' work, the arm picks up muscle signals generated in the natural stump, transmits these to a small amplifier and uses them to drive a compact electric motor. A force-sensing feedback element detects changes in weight and adjusts voltage levels accordingly, so that the arm exerts neither too little nor too much power when coping with any given object. This sort of dynamic feedback closely mimics the natural feedback loop. All of this machinery is housed inside a flesh-colored fiberglass casing that resembles a real arm.

The Boston arm currently uses a hook-type hand but plans are under way to link the limb to one of the articulated British hands. Then, says Dr. Glimcher, "the next stage is research in the nerves that carry impulses from the brain to the muscles." By carefully mapping out the nerve signals, he observes, and using them directly rather than by going through the muscles, it will be possible to achieve even greater control in artificial hands and arms. "It can be done," he says. "It's a matter of development."

The most important part of the Boston arm (and of others like it, such as the one developed at the Temple University School of Medicine in Philadelphia) is a pattern-recognition circuit. It is here that the mini-impulses picked up by the external electrodes on the stump are sorted out. On the basis of their power and origin, among other things, the circuit is able to decide just what it is that the brain is commanding. Then it translates these commands electronically via the various small motors within the arm. One of the great advantages of this system over older ones is that the individual need not spend months or, as happens in some cases, even years adjusting to it. It does most of the work automatically, requiring little of its host.

Sophisticated as these systems are, they leave something to be desired in that the external electrodes upon which they rely are not the most selective sensors. There is a "noise" problem generated by signals from adjacent muscles with which the system should not be concerned. To circumvent this problem, researchers at the Powered Limbs Unit of West Hendon Hospital in Britain have come up with what amounts to an implantable electrode or transmitter called an Emgor. It uses a resonator circuit that does not require batteries to detect myoelectric signals, thus obviating the need for frequent surgical intervention to replenish the power source. With such systems, it is expected, amputees will even be capable of unconscious gesticulations. In other words, they will not even have to exert themselves by "thinking" their limbs into action. When an incisive "chop" in the air with an arm is called for to help punctuate an emphatic oral point, the chop will simply materialize.

Similar lower body prostheses have also been developed; Soviets again lead the field with development of a myoelectric leg. More extensive lower body prostheses, though crude, have at least advanced to the point that doctors, in some cases, are willing to perform what have come to be known as *hemicorporectomies—amputation of the entire lower half of the body,* including legs, rectum, genitalia, etc. The radical procedure was offered to patients in a New York hospital as an alternative to death from abdominal cancer. Not all of them took it. Some preferred death to the gross mutilation required by the procedure; others were apparently dissatisfied with the nature of the prosthetic replacement. It seems logical to assume that, with more sophisticated knowledge of the nervous system than is presently available, artificial legs can be made to operate myoelectrically even in the absence of any leg stumps; ultimately even artificial genitalia might be endowed with something approximating natural function, once they are appropriately wired into the nervous system.

"TICKLE TALK"

For those handicapped in other ways—the deaf, the mute, the blind and the paralyzed—there are a number of new cybernetic systems. "Tickle talk" is the name that has been applied to a variety of cutaneous communications systems that could prove of immense value to the blind. One of these systems enables sightless individuals to "see" with the skin of their backs! A small TV camera acts as the "eye," picking up images in front of the blind person. It converts the images (chairs, telephones, other people, etc.) into a pattern of dots which correspond to the actual objects being viewed. These patterns are channeled electronically through a computerlike machine that activates a number of tiny Teflon-tipped cones that vibrate against the skin of the back, permitting the individual to *feel* the dot pattern and thus perceive the images that are being picked up by the TV eye. Though it sounds complex, all of this happens almost instantaneously.

Developed by Dr. Paul Bach-y-Rita, a neurophysiologist, and Dr. Carter Collins, a bio-physicist, at San Francisco's Pacific Medical Center, the "tickle-talk" system requires little training. In less than ten hours most blind subjects are able to "see" simple objects. First they learn to discriminate between vertical, horizontal and curved lines. Then they go on to master geometric shapes such as circles, squares, triangles. From there it's just a short step to recognizing whole objects, such as telephones, human hands, chairs, etc.

Interestingly, the subject, once accustomed to the system, tends to forget that he is "seeing" through his back; despite the still unwieldy size of the system, the man-machine symbiosis is really quite remarkable. The subject even begins to judge distances, by noting changes in size and position of objects. "When we use the zoom lens to move in on objects," Dr. Bach-y-Rita observes, "the student ducks because he thinks the object is moving at him!"

The San Francisco team plans to bring out a portable, battery-powered model of the tickle-talk system. It will include a tiny TV camera that will be worn, rather like a miner's lamp, on the head and a special "undershirt" equipped with hundreds of electrodes to convey the tactile image. Estimated cost per system is somewhere in the neighborhood of a thousand dollars.

Dr. Herbert Schimmel, a physicist at the Albert Einstein College of Medicine in New York, makes the stunning prediction that tickle talk will be succeeded—possibly within five to ten years—by *a television camera small enough to fit in the eye socket*. Electronic signals from these implanted cameras will be transmitted to wires implanted in the brain within the visual cortex, which, in normally sighted individuals, sorts out impulses from the eye. Mechanically augmented in this way, the cortex will do the same for the blind, permitting the brain to translate the electrical impulses into images, providing sight, complete with motion, depth and color, where there was none before. (More on this in the chapter on electronic stimulation of the brain.)

Another cutaneous sighting system frees the blind from the confines of Braille. Developed by electrical engineer John G. Linvill (whose daughter is blind) and a team of researchers at Stanford University and Stanford Research Institute, the Opticon (or Optical Tactical Converter) transforms conventionally printed letters into letters than can be *felt*. The Opticon simply scans the printed material (whether it be a novel or a typed letter from a friend) and then transmits what it "sees" to a vibrating alphabet unit on which the subject rests one finger; letters are then outlined, via a matrix of vibrating "pins," on the tip of the finger. The transmission rate is controlled by the subject, who moves a pencillike electronic probe along the line undergoing "translation." If he speeds up, so does the vibrator. Material is kept in place by the machine. It is expected that subjects will be able to read at rates comparable to their Braille rate, possibly faster, but now they will also be able to read *anything* in print, rather than limit themselves to Braille publications. Cost of the machines is expected to be that of inexpensive TV sets.

Code-Com is another device in this family of prosthetic aids, but one designed for the deaf as well as the blind. Its developer, Western Electric, reports that "deaf and deaf-blind people will be able to 'talk' by tapping out a code on a small plate built into the phone. Each time the plate is tapped, the phone sends out a tone that travels over the regular telephone lines. And at the other end, the Code-Com phone translates this tone into a blinking light for the deaf who can see, or a vibrating plate that the deaf-blind can feel with their fingers. A blinking light also tells sighted people they have a phone call; air current from a small electric fan signals a deaf-blind person."

For the more seriously handicapped, such as those missing all their limbs, for those almost entirely paralyzed and so on, there are a variety of new telecommunications systems. Haig Kafafian, president and research director of the non-profit Cybernetics Research Institute, has developed a series of man-machine devices that go by such names as "Cybercom," "Cybertype," "Cyberphone," "Cyber-Tone" and "Cybertac." They are variously designed for the deaf, mute, blind, for amputees, victims of paralysis and cerebral palsy and so on. The machines are adaptable, permitting operation via whatever bodily motions, however crude, the individual is still capable of performing. Some can be operated by pressure from the head, others by pressure from an arm or leg, from an artificial limb, even by pressure from the tongue. Some "tongue typers" can go at speeds up to a hundred words per minute when equipped with small mouth-held "keyboards."

TELESURGERY AND TELEPSYCHIATRY

It should be apparent by now that the ways in which man and machine can unite harmoniously are legion. But before concluding our examination of the medical cyborg, we should take a brief look at some of the opportunities for using machines to assist in the diagnosis and treatment of man's ills. Though machines, in this category, are not called on to form permanent unions with man, they do open yet another channel for the peaceful coexistence of man and machine, of human software and computer hardware.

Before turning ourselves over to the computer psychoanalyst, let's study a no less intriguing but considerably less formidable system, one pioneered at Massachusetts General Hospital and Boston Logan International Airport. A two-way closed-circuit TV system links the two centers, making possible something doctors call "telediagnosis." It was developed by Dr. Kenneth T. Bird of Massachusetts General and Richard Oldham of WGBH-TV. It permits a doctor to examine and diagnose a patient from across a distance of miles or even thousands of miles, a great boon to the oversubscribed practitioner who can now spend more time in the office and less unproductive time on the road; a great boon to the patient, too, who will increasingly be able to count on "seeing" a doctor on short, emergency notice—again without having to travel to the doctor's office itself. One stresses the word "increasingly" since, at present, there are still few telediagnosis systems in operation. They are, however, likely to proliferate rapidly.

The Boston system is of sufficient quality that a physician can literally look down the throat of his distant patient when he says "Ahhh." In addition, the system comes equipped with a number of electronic sensing devices which can easily be attached to the patient by a nurse at the remote station or even by a chance bystander under instructions from the doctor. The Logan station is presently equipped with instruments to check blood pressure, heart, pulse and respiration rates, and to analyze electrocardiograms and X rays gathered at the scene.

Telediagnosis could do much to alleviate problems arising because of the acute world-wide doctor shortage, Dr. Bird notes, observing that nurses and other paramedical personnel would be adequate to man telediagnosis stations in rural and suburban communities, relying upon practiced physicians in major metropolitan hospitals to diagnose the patient and provide, when needed, instructions for emergency treatment. The system can also save time, and probably lives, when added to ambulance equipment, something that has already been initiated by several California hospitals. In most emergencies, doctors need an electrocardiogram (ECG) in order to judge adequately the condition of the patient. To save time, ambulance attendants from some California hospitals are trained to attach chest electrodes to the patient even as he is being prepared for transport to the hospital. Then, en route, the electronic ECG signals are telemetered to the emergency room, so that by the time the patient arrives there doctors have already analyzed his condition.

In Britain, two Edinburgh hospitals are linked with a telediagnosis system so that medical consultations concerning difficult cases can be carried out without the physical assembling of the consultants in question. The system has even been used to enable a senior doctor to help a beginner through a surgical procedure, providing him with a "blow by blow" set of instructions.

It appears that telediagnosis is but a precursor to actual *telesurgery,* in which it would be possible for a doctor at one corner of the world to operate on a patient at the opposite corner. Such a system will require electronically "slaving" a set of sophisticated

133

mechanical manipulators at the remote site to the arms of the physician so that he can literally reach around the world if necessary. Utopian as this sounds, such systems are a distant possibility for the near future, and, in fact, mechanical manipulators that mimic even the most subtle movement of the human arms to which they are "slaved" by wireless electronic signals across vast expanses of space are now in existence and will be examined in the next chapter. It is even possible now to conceive of a whole team of doctors, each in a different country, joining together via telesurgical circuits to operate on a difficult surgical case.

Ultimately, it is likely that computers will be called in to help handle the immense amount of data that will flow through the teletherapy network, and possibly even the decisions involved in the composition of telesurgical teams will be left to the judgment of the computer, since it will quickly and objectively be able to size up the combination of talent that can most optimally cope with any given situation. Possibly, too, in the more distant future, such systems will give rise to a new international medical code of ethics in which "being on call" will imply an obligation to answer, despite racial, national or political identity, the commands of the computer. In the event that a surgeon selected by the computer is already engaged in the operating room (or on another telesurgical circuit) the computer will get a "busy signal" and automatically "ring" its second choice.

The system, of course, need not be restricted to surgery. In fact, telediagnosis has already given rise to *telepsychiatry*. This, too, got its start at Massachusetts General Hospital. This time the system was linked to Bedford Veterans' Administration Hospital eighteen miles distant. "Interactive TV" is the name given the system by Dr. Thomas Dwyer, the psychiatrist who serves as coordinator of the project. The system permits both psychiatrist and patient to view each other while they talk, and the doctor is equipped with a zoom lens so that he can "move in" on his patient for a closer view—but without letting the patient know it.

THE COMPUTER AS PHYSICIAN AND PSYCHIATRIST

Dr. Simon Ramo, one of the founders of Thompson Ramo Woolldridge, Inc., and former chief scientist of America's intercontinental ballistic missile program, writes as follows in the *Proceedings of the IRE:* "How many physicians can your doctor consult with? A practical answer would most often be: maybe two or three. The physician in the future technological age, toward which we are in such rapid transition, will routinely introduce his data on a patient to this network of 'consultative wisdom.' The patient's entire past history, the results of all tests, the symptoms and complaints, and even a statement of the family background of inherited tendencies—all of this would be efficiently introduced to the medical intellectronics system."

"Intellectronics" is a Ramo invention, coined to describe the extension of man's intellect by electronics, specifically by computerized telecommunications and teleanalysis of data. Such systems, Dr. Ramo continues, "will quickly react to give the doctor not all, but key portions of what would have been the result of many consultations with other physicians. It will call out questions and possibilities our physician may not have asked himself. It will give statistical probabilities (because it will have the amassed data to do so) of the relative effectiveness of various treatments—with numerous variations and warnings to account for corollary possibilities and complications, all automatically turned up within the machine, triggered by some of the detailed data that the physician introduced about the patient. With diseases nationally monitored, the statistical approach to medical practice will take on an entirely new stature. Cause-and-effect relationships will be studied on a large but rapid scale, tying ailment to treatment. And again it will raise the intellectual effort of our physicians."

Dr. Ramo believes that medical and psychoanalytical intellectronics of this order of sophistication will be

135

upon us shortly after the turn of the century. "Behavioral engineering" or "behavioral electronics" are now established concepts, utilizing numerous "behavior-modifying machines." One of the earliest of these (1904) was the electric blanket, designed to discourage bed-wetters by giving them a shock at the appropriate moment. The device proved its worth and today still exists, though in more elegant form: the electric pad now activates a tape recording at the first trace of urine that instructs the child that it is time to get up. If the child does not respond (by turning off a switch), mild electric shock ensues. Similar behavior-modifying devices have been designed to suppress smoking, nail biting, poor posture, nervous tics, even homosexuality and obsessional thoughts.

Dr. Ramo's "intellectronics" concept, of course, goes far beyond this sort of machine-aided therapy. He envisions a ubiquitous computer presence to monitor psychic and physical health from birth on. A team at the Otolaryngological Institute of McGill University Medical School, led by Dr. R. P. Gannon, has, in fact, already utilized a computer in diagnosing ailments during the earliest days of human life. A digital LINC-8 computer is being used by the McGill group to detect deafness in the newborn.

The baby is typically exposed to intervals of noise created by a computer-controlled audiometer alternated with equal intervals of silence. The computer determines the amount of hearing function in the infant by comparing heart rate during the silent and noisy phases. In a totally deaf infant there will be no difference in heart rate whatever between the two periods. Until the computer was called in there was no sure way of detecting deafness or partial deafness very early in development. The new diagnostic technique is important because it permits doctors to gauge the scope of the hearing deficit and to provide appropriate auditory stimuli. Without such stimuli, that portion of the brain associated with hearing *and speaking* fails to develop; with it, the child, though he may never hear perfectly, is given all the help possible and stands a good chance of at least learning to speak properly.

While on the subject of babies, *having them* is another area that may ultimately come under the survey of the computer analyst. Geneticists Harold P. Klinger and Orlando J. Miller, speaking before an international symposium on fetology (treatment of the fetus), suggested that what is badly needed in this country is a national registry of hereditary abnormalities to help prevent conception of defective children. If such a registry were to become a reality it would probably work something like this:

At birth, skin or blood samples would, as a matter of course and, indeed, as a matter of law, be fed into a computerized genetic scanner. The scanner would quickly establish the presence of any chromosomal anomalies and print them out on data cards that would be kept on permanent file in Washington, D.C. When two people applied for a marriage license, their respective cards would again be scanned—this time in conjunction with one another. If found to be genetically compatible, they would be provided with authorization to undergo a second scan (to see if any postnatal changes had occurred, as a result of exposure to dangerous drugs, radiation, etc.). If they were still "clean" they would then be authorized to marry.

A number of scientists, including Nobel laureates Sir Peter Medawar, Francis Crick and Linus Pauling, believe that incompatible persons should be restrained by law from marrying one another or, in any event, from having children with one another. Dr. Pauling has suggested, only half in jest, that people who carry defective genes should have that information tattooed on their foreheads. Dr. Crick has stated that having children "ought to be as much a matter of public concern as driving a car," something that required a license years ago.

When I pointed out some of the possible advantages of a national registry of hereditary abnormalities on a New York talk show, the program's host expressed amazement and shock, protesting that this was computerized "invasion of privacy" and that it would "take all the love out of marriage." When you meet an attractive girl, he went on, "it's all right to be curious about her figure, but to ask about her genes—that would be awful!"

This is an understandable emotional reaction. But it doesn't stand up to reason. Having your genes analyzed by a computer, in the first place, is really no more an invasion of privacy than having your heartbeat analyzed by a doctor with a stethoscope. Nor is it any more an invasion of privacy than having your urine tested for glucose, your blood tested for evidence of venereal disease (already required almost everywhere in order to get a marriage license). All of these things are done for the good of the individual and for the protection of society.

Equally nonsensical is the idea that the computer will take all the love out of marriage. Surely the individual who would take the time and effort to ensure that any children he might have would be healthy exhibits far more love for his offspring than does the individual who scorns such precautions as too "calculating" and "unromantic." As one geneticist put it, "There's nothing very romantic about a mongoloid child, a cleft palate or a deformed body."

True, with the advent of computer gene-scanning, girl watching may be in for some new twists as redblooded voyeurs begin showing as much interest in internal dimension as they now show for the external ones. "I love her but our number 11 chromosomes clash" could become the stuff of tragedy—and soap opera—in the not so distant future.

Even in the down-to-earth present, Dr. Nathan S. Kline, one of the most esteemed figures in psychiatric research, is able to call the computer "the most important development in psychiatric treatment since drug therapy." Computers designed for use at Dr. Kline's Rockland State Mental Hospital in New York take massive amounts of statistical data and convert it into readable, concise, constantly up-to-date reports on the status and progress of mental patients. With the push of a button the doctor can have at his fingertips all of the pertinent information he needs on any given patient. In the past, he would probably have had to plow through numerous case history reports on the patient, some of them three or four inches thick; each would probably have been prepared by a different individual, making for a lack of continuity, and each would probably have omitted at least one or two critical bits of data.

What follows is an excerpt from a computer-written report (prepared from various check lists, describing, in fragmented form, patient progress):

"The present episode, with no apparent precipitating factor, has an onset of more than one month and has lasted one to five years. . . . There have been four previous episodes. . . . Hospitalization was never required in the past. There has been no attempt at suicide. . . . The patient was never arrested. . . . The family has an accepting attitude with regard to the patient's illness. Concerning prior treatments, she has had antidepressant drugs and supportive psychotherapy."

Dr. Kline is also using the computer to help sort out subtle information that evades normal clinical observation of the most difficult mental cases. For example, he has computer technicians—stationed on one side of one-way windows—constantly watching a group of chronic schizophrenics who have resisted all forms of drug treatment. The technicians channel all of their observations of these patients (even those that would seem irrelevant) into the computer. Dr. Kline hopes that the computer will be able to use this data to discover distinct categories of mental illness within what presently *appears* to be but one large category. Such categorical refinements could well open the way to new avenues of treatment where none exists now. Dr. Kline hopes, too, that the computer can be used to establish *trends* of mental illness, by analyzing case histories, city-wide and even world-wide. To that end, he is now trying to persuade psychiatrists in countries around the world to record their findings and case histories in NOVEL, the language of his psychiatric computers.

Dr. Kline expects that before too long computers will begin to provide doctors with a list of possible diagnoses in each individual case. Eventually, say some bio-engineers, computer and brain will be directly linked. "The information which a machine can obtain and store from a person in a few minutes," says R. M. Page of the U. S. Naval Research Laboratory, "will exceed the fruits of a lifetime of man-to-man communication. The machine will operate in the realms of the physical, psychological and biological. Its functions will be to diagnose, prescribe and treat. . . . In the psychological realm, it will analyze personality and diagnose psychiatric problems. It will prescribe courses of action appropriate to personality and, by repeated suggestion and testing, effect psychiatric cures.

"In the medical realm," he continues, "it will diagnose illness and the tendency to disease. It will prescribe cures and map the course to sustained health. It will in some cases give the required treatments. The coupling mechanisms to carry out all these functions will be myriad, including in some cases electrical connections to the body and to the brain. Some connections may be wireless, with imperceptible transmitting elements implanted in the body."

THREE

REACHING
FOR THE STARS

THE NEW ERA
OF PARTICIPANT EVOLUTION

I suppose one could call a man in an iron lung a cyborg, but the concept has far wider implications than that. One day we may be able to enter into temporary unions with any sufficiently sophisticated machines, thus being able not merely to control but to become *a spaceship or a submarine or a TV network.*

—Arthur C. Clarke
in *Profiles of the Future*

In the past, the altering of bodily functions to suit different environments was accomplished through evolution. From now on, at least in some degree, this can be achieved without alteration of heredity by suitable bio-chemical, physiological and electronic modification of man's existing modus vivendi.

—Dr. Manfred Clynes and
Dr. Nathan S. Kline
in a paper entitled "Cyborgs and
Space" published in *Astronautics*

All true progress is progress in love.
—Dr. Manfred Clynes,
Director, Bio-cybernetics Laboratory,
Rockland State Hospital

The cyborg—an evolutionary chimera one step in advance of man—has already burst out of the confines of the medical arena into the world at large. In a laboratory on the banks of the Hudson River he communicates flesh-and-blood perceptions through a computer, to which he is linked, without words or even rudimentary gestures; at another laboratory—this one in England—he stops and starts complex machines simply by "willing" them into action or inaction; at a neuropsychiatric institute in San Francisco and a research center in Southern California he instantaneously projects his emotions onto a motion picture screen via a meaningful matrix of coded colors and, utilizing this cerebral drama, learns to exercise complete command over his state of mind (see Chapter Five).

Still other cyborgs—once ordinary human beings—kill whatever they look at with the mere flick of an eye or, with the same minute exertion, bring an automobile to a grinding halt. Some cyborgs are so "wired" that they can relive past experiences with such vividness that they are unable to distinguish the synthetic experience from the real; others are able to evoke in their own bodies—at will and at a moment's notice—pleasure so profound and all-pervasive that it surpasses anything known to ordinary man (Chapter Four).

The possibilities for the cyborg are truly stunning, as suggested in the passage quoted at the head of this chapter in which Arthur C. Clarke, the writer and astrophysicist, expresses his belief that the cyborg, initially a medical phenomenon, is bound for the stars. "The thrill that can be obtained from driving a racing car or flying an airplane may be only a pale ghost of the excitement our great-grandchildren may know," he continues, "when the individual human consciousness is free to roam at will from machine to machine, through all the reaches of sea and sky and space."

Space, as much as medicine, has fostered the cyborg concept; in fact, it was in connection with the space challenge that the word itself was coined. Dr. Manfred Clynes and Dr. Nathan Kline, whom we met in the last chapter, both of Rockland State Hospital in New York, first introduced the word in a paper presented at the Psychophysiological Aspects of Space Flight Symposium in San Antonio several years ago. They noted that "in the past, the altering of bodily functions to suit different environments was accomplished through evolution. From now on, at least in some degree, this can be achieved without alteration of heredity by suitable bio-chemical, physiological and electronic modification of man's existing *modus vivendi*."

The value of this sort of "participant evolution," they pointed out, could be immense, particularly in the space-effort, where a self-regulating man-machine system could function so much better than a conventional astronaut. "What are some of the devices necessary for creating self-regulating man-machine systems?" they asked. "This self-regulation needs to function without the benefit of consciousness, in order to cooperate with the body's own autonomous homeostatic controls. For the artificially extended homeostatic control system functioning unconsciously, one of us [Manfred Clynes] has coined the term *cyborg*."

THE CYBERNAUT AND PARTICIPANT EVOLUTION

Instead of lugging along into outerspace extensive and encumbering artificial environments compatible with the present model of man, the two doctors asked, why not *change* man so that he would himself be compatible with the new environment? The astronautic cyborg they envisioned would be considerably more agile and certainly far more effective than our present-day moon men. For one thing, the cyborg's space suit would be lightweight and skin tight. It would require no pressurization since the cyborg's lungs would be partially collapsed and the blood in them artificially cooled. Mouth and nose would be superfluous and hence sealed and totally non-functioning. Respiration and most other bodily processes would be affected cybernetically through the utilization of artificial organs and sensors, some of which would be attached to the exterior of the suit while others would be implanted surgically within the cyborg's body. These computerized components would serve to maintain constant pressure, temperature and metabolism within the body, despite external environmental fluctuations.

The cybernaut, according to this visualization, would travel through space in a low-cost, unsealed cabin, free to move about the wastes of Mars and the moon unmindful of radical alterations in temperature and unencumbered by heavy equipment. Chemical molecules and concentrated foods constantly spilling into the blood stream would nourish and protect him. Wastes, of course, would be recycled to make new foods, and communications would be carried on by radio propagation of electronic impulses originating in the vocal cords.

Dr. Michael Del Duca, a former NASA scientist, takes the cybernaut conception entirely seriously and, in fact, has enlarged upon it. He believes that man will eventually learn how to convert sunlight directly into energy within his own body. This sort of photosynthetic cyborg, he says, will not need any food at all and will be free to spend his entire life exploring the depths of the ocean or the far reaches of space.

The notion that man can now adapt himself, almost at will, to changing environments or simply to changing fashions, to participate in his own evolution, got a number of hefty boosts beginning in the 1940s, when it was firmly established that deoxyribonucleic acid (better known simply as DNA) is the very essence of life, the residing place of all heredity, the chemical template of creation. DNA is the innermost stuff of the chromosomes, genes and nucleotides, the wondrously complex structures that determine not only the grosser characteristics of our being (whether four-legged, two-legged or no-legged) but also the finest and most intimate details (red wings, blue eyes, moles).

The delineation of the DNA structure in the 1950s —by Dr. Francis H. C. Crick and Dr. James Watson, both of whom have since been awarded the Nobel Prize for their achievements—and the illumination of many of its inner workings in the 1960s, primarily by Dr. Marshall Nirenberg, have truly set the stage for the premier performance of a new creator: man. With the genetic code of life rapidly yielding its secrets to the decipherers, a new era is dawning in which man will have at his disposal the means of remaking himself in images limited perhaps only by his imagination or according to the dictates of a new or changing environment.

Possibly, as the world grows "smaller" owing to the crush of the population, man will find it advantageous to make *himself* smaller; as he moves into the oceans, perhaps he will want to incorporate gills and other aquatic appurtenances into his genotype; similarly, as he moves out into the far reaches of space, he may wish to redesign his body in such a way that he will be able to cope with the requirements of this new world without recourse to life-support systems, created at great costs in efficiency and mobility, to reconcile incompatibilities of organism and environment.

At an international symposium on The Future of Man held in London several years ago, the world-renowned geneticist-philosopher Dr. J. B. S. Haldane looked ahead to the day when it will be possible to engineer man's characteristics according to the needs of society. Discoursing on the varied requirements of extraterrestrial environments, Dr. Haldane observed that "a gibbon is better suited than a man for life in a low gravitational field, such as that of a spaceship, an asteroid, or perhaps even the moon. A platyrrhine with a prehensile tail is even more so. Gene grafting may make it possible to incorporate such features into the human stock."

Dr. Haldane had other proposals. For long space journeys, legs would be just so much dead weight; thus, he said, it might be best to breed legless astronauts for the first space flight to the stars, "thus reducing not only their weight but their food and oxygen requirements. A regressive mutation to the condition of our ancestors in the mid-Pliocene, with prehensile feet, that can grasp things, no appreciable heels and an ape-like pelvis, would be still better." For high-gravitational fields, such as will ultimately be encountered on such planets as Jupiter, he suggested that astronauts be bred for short legs and squat bodies. Perhaps, he observed, they should even be quadrupedal, adding, "I would back an achondroplastic [dwarf] against a normal man on Jupiter."

Among other "controlled mutations" foreseen by Dr. Haldane is the "aseptic" man, germ-free inside and out. This future cousin, he declared, could be a boon to germ-free planets but might otherwise prove troublesome, particularly whenever forced to come into contact with humans such as ourselves who enjoy close symbiotic relationships with millions upon millions of external and internal microbes. "To an aseptic person, producing among other things inodorous feces," Dr. Haldane pointed out, "the rest of humanity will appear as stinkers and there will be grave emotional tensions, including a sexual barrier."

Advances in the field of molecular biology have come so quickly of late that a good many scientists now believe that "genetic engineering" may be only two decades away. Already scientists are learning how to put genes together in the test tube and how to synthesize their elemental components. Microsurgical techniques provide one means of altering the natural material. Experiments with special viruses point to still other ways of doing the same thing; it appears that certain viruses, adept at insinuating their ways into the cells, can be made to freight in with them specially prepared genetic instructions (in the form of carefully prepared DNA nucleotide sequences), thus altering the course of development in the desired direction.

"We can be optimistic about long-range possibilities of therapy by the design and synthesis and introduction of new genes or gene products into cells of defective organs," declares Dr. Edward Tatum, the Nobel laureate who coined the term "genetic surgery." Another pioneer in this field, Dr. Marshall Nirenberg, is similarly optimistic: "My guess is that cells will be programmed with synthesized messages within twenty-five years." And Dr. Joshua Lederberg, yet another Nobel Prize winner, predicts genetic surgery within the next two decades, perhaps sooner with an all-out effort.

Where will "participant evolution" lead? Some of the possibilities, such as Dr. Haldane's engineered space mutants, have already been discussed. *Science Journal,* a British publication, asked its readers, most of them scientists, what they would do, given the opportunity to redesign the human body. A writer from Manchester University suggested that the human female be restructured in such a way that she would lay eggs, which could either be hatched—"or eaten for breakfast." Others called for gills and other underwater apparatus, while some pointed to the utility of an enlarged caecum (the sac containing the vermiform appendix) containing bacteria able to transform cellulose into food; cows presently come equipped with this undeniably economical capability. One reader wanted everyone programmed with photographic memories and another proposed that the male be redesigned so that his vulnerable testes are tucked away inside the body.

Similar suggestions for the remaking of man were forthcoming in *Sciences,* a publication of the New York Academy of Sciences. Among them was one by Dr. Charles H. Townes, the Nobel Prize-winning physicist who developed the principles underlying development of the laser. "Man," he said, "should be smaller in

148

size and have a much longer life cycle than in the past. . . . In the past, man's size needed to be reasonably large so that he could exert the physical force necessary to do work and fight enemies; the application of intelligence and the development of tools has completely changed this. . . . Small size and long life would, of course, very much facilitate long space journeys, to mention one of man's most recent challenges."

Dr. Dominic Recaldin of London University had a similarly ingenious plan for future man: "We should take a lesson in self-sufficiency from the plants," he wrote, "and learn the art of photosynthesis before our greedy teeth pick the planet clean. With chlorophyll beneath their skins, men could unchain themselves forever from the soil."

Some of the most far-reaching suggestions forthcoming in these surveys went beyond genetic engineering to bio-cybernetic engineering and the cyborg concept. The suggestion, for example, that man be linked directly to computers to enhance mental efficiency provides "participant evolution" with a new dimension. Indeed, some insist that bio-cybernetics offers a far greater degree of participation than genetics; the coupling of man and machine can provide instantaneous and, as Dr. Clynes points out, possibly *reversible,* modification of the genotype, whereas controlled biological change is apt to take a good deal longer and to prove permanent, at least in individual cases.

Still, the genetic and the cybernetic are really complementary aspects of participant evolution, and, as pointed out in the introduction, it would be a mistake to try to establish a genes/machines dichotomy. Genetic manipulation in many cases may be a necessary prerequisite to effective man-machine coupling. Genetic surgery may prove useful, for example, in altering bodily proportions to fit the dimensions of a mechanical system better. Similarly, it might prove useful in encouraging the body to accept readily foreign implants, such as electronic circuitry, artificial organs and the like.

Ironically, genetic and bio-cybernetic engineering

might place man on the brink of his own obsolescence, for they are the tools by which he will replace himself with a new order of life—the cybernetic organism. No wonder participant evolution has been hailed by Dr. Tatum as "the most astounding prospect so far suggested by science" and by Dr. Robert L. Sinsheimer as "one of the most important concepts to arise in the history of mankind." Because so much has already been written about the genetic part of this concept, what follows is concerned primarily with the cybernetic, with the mechanical amplification and transmogrification of man.

COPULATING "COMPUTERS"

Since coining the term "cyborg" in 1960, Dr. Clynes, director of the Rockland State Hospital Bio-cybernetics Laboratory (dedicated to the computerized study of biological control systems that operate without conscious awareness in the individual), internationally acclaimed concert pianist and inventor of the widely used CAT computer, has continued to develop his concept. "The important thing to remember about the cyborg," he reflects, "is that as man changes he may no longer have at his disposal the ordinary means of expressing his humanity. So if he is to remain truly human, he must find some substitute means of expressing his humanity." This means that man must first understand the essential qualities of "humanness." What is the essence of a smile, of hate, of love? Can these things be defined and distilled?

Dr. Clynes' startling answer is *yes!* His studies have demonstrated that all of our perceptions and emotions have specific, measurable time-space shapes. When two or more people look at the color red they all produce the same sort of brain potentials or signals. These can be detected by delicate sensors and analyzed by a computer. Our emotions, similarly, are related to specific brain potentials so that, as has also been demonstrated in Dr. Clynes' laboratory, computers can now literally read our minds.

When we can no longer talk, smile, breathe or gesture (assuming for the purpose of this discussion that we may someday be contained not only in cybernautic capsules but perhaps even in little metal boxes) we will *still* be able to convey our humanity—by electronically transmitting the desired potentials to the other little metal boxes with whom we are desirous of communication. Hence, as we lose our limbs, our faces, and all our other flesh-and-blood parts, Dr. Clynes says, we need not lose the wealth of expressions, gestures, smiles and inflections of voice that set us apart from and presumably above the rest of the creatures of the earth. In the future, "good vibrations" will almost certainly be more than just an expression.

And, Dr. Clynes points out, an understanding of the nature of our thoughts, in terms of their mathematical, electronic and time-space (shape) identities, will permit us to communicate *better* than we do at the present time. "We may even find new shapes," he adds, "and discover means of utilizing them to communicate in entirely new ways—ways that cannot even be imagined now."

Along with a growing number of computer experts, Dr. Clynes does not believe that intelligence need be confined to the DNA structure. "I believe that life is more a matter of relationships and organization than of material," he asserts. His conception of the intelligent, conscious computer is really a vision of the ultimate cyborg—humanity in an entirely new organizational package that may not contain a single DNA molecule. Whatever its components, he says, it is as "human" as man so long as the essential inner shapes of man's psychic being and some means of transmitting them are retained. In so far, of course, as it is capable of entirely new forms of expression, it becomes "superhuman," defining a new, dominant rung on the evolutionary ladder.

Dr. Clynes is a man who believes that "all true progress is progress in love." Hence his lyrical, somewhat whimsical vision of the ultimate cyborg, man's humanness embodied in a computer-like package, is not surprising: "It seems likely that if computers [as defined in the special sense above] can control their condition of awareness and optimize it with greater ease than we can in our present form, they will prefer the state of love. Since one of the characteristics of love is the desire to join with the object of love, the computers loving each other would want to merge. This will be less of a problem for computers than it is for people and will have the advantage that a combined computer could be a little better than each separately.

"There will arise, then, a succession of merging computers until there will be one enormous computer in a state of bliss, contemplating the order of nature. If this state should become difficult to maintain in time the computer would have the choice of subdividing itself and reverting to the previous condition of multiple individuals who love each other and would tend to merge again. We actually face then a playful state of oscillation in which individuals unite and divide and subdivide in ever new combinations and forms. Strangely, such an image is merely an analog of nature as we see it today."

CREATURES OF RADIATION—BEYOND 2001

Arthur C. Clarke, in many ways, goes even further than Dr. Clynes in his conception of the future cyborg. His philosophy on the subject, as we shall see, pervades the film *2001: A Space Odyssey,* which still continues to delight and *confuse* viewers as few films ever have. To prepare ourselves for Clarke's vision of the future, it is perhaps best to begin by examining the man himself, an opportunity presented to me shortly after release of *2001* (based on his short story "The Sentinel" and cocreated by himself and director Stanley Kubrick).

"The only way to define the limits of the possible is by going beyond them into the impossible." That's

Clarke's Second Law. In it is all the daring optimism and imagination that have made its author such a dazzling success. In the realm of the "possible," Clarke's lucid and authoritative non-fiction has made the complexities that challenge man in two great frontiers— the world of space and the depths of the sea—meaningful to millions of people around the globe. In the realm of the "impossible," where he feels most comfortable, Clarke is the self-proclaimed and undisputed doyen of science fiction writers. But it is prophetic vision that gives life to his facts and a firm footing in reality that informs his fiction. In the embrace of Clarke's cosmic broad-mindedness, science fact and science fiction, once light-years apart, seem to meld into one.

To date, more than five million copies of Clarke's forty books have been printed in thirty languages. Lift-off for the writer-scientist was publication of *Interplanetary Flight* twenty years ago. The book, which described in technical detail the intricacies of astronautics and the era that was about to dawn, is still selling today. It was in 1945 that Clarke wrote and published in *Wireless World* the article that established him as one of the foremost thinkers in space technology. The article called "Extraterrestrial Relays" is often credited with having started the communications-satellite business. The article described *in precise detail* the synchronous communications satellite which became a reality twenty years later with Comsat. Understandably, Clarke calls the short non-fiction article "the most important thing I've written or ever will write."

In *Profiles of the Future,* another non-fiction work, Clarke, who holds first-class honor degrees in physics and math from King's College in London, with graduate work in applied astronomy, startled many of his readers with his provocative predictions: contact with extraterrestrials by 2030, creation of artificial life by 2060, immortality by 2090, etc.

In *The Promise of Space,* Clarke sums up all of his scientific writings on the space challenge. If anything characterizes the book, it is his refusal to be cowed by the incredible obstacles that seem to stand between man and the conquest of space. He not only envisions construction of cities in the hostile environments of our nearest planetary neighbors but also foresees the day when man will venture out beyond the solar system at velocities that break the so-called universal speed limit, the speed of light. Here Clarke's First Law would seem in order:

"When a distinguished but elderly scientist states that something is impossible, he is very probably wrong." He defines "elderly" thus: "In physics, mathematics and astronautics, it means over thirty; in the other disciplines, senile decay is sometimes postponed to the forties." What this boils down to, as far as Clarke is concerned, is that "anything that is theoretically possible will be achieved in practice, no matter what the technical difficulties, if it is desired greatly enough."

Among the things Clarke foresees are long space odysseys to the distant stars. He notes that "interstellar flight is not an engineering problem but a medical one." It is simply the problem of keeping people alive during the long journey. Apart from the more obvious possible solutions provided by hibernation, cryogenic freezing and other approaches to suspended animation, Clarke foresees another possibility of getting around the problem of damning generations of travelers to life in space. Instead of sending people, he proposes that we simply send the germ cells, fertilize them with the aid of computers some twenty years before the voyage is to end, "carry the embryos through to birth by techniques already foreshadowed in today's biology labs—and bring up the babies under the tutelage of cybernetic nurses who would teach them their inheritance and their destiny." (Computers capable of all this would have to be the great-grandchildren of Hal, the would-be hero of *2001*, but such computers appear to be on the way.)

Promise of Space, incidentally, is supposedly Clarke's *last* non-fiction book. After its appearance he said that he planned to turn entirely to science fiction (though he did take time out to write about the first moon landing). Why? "Well, there's the Clarke-Asimov Treaty for one thing. My half of the treaty is that I tell everyone that Isaac Asimov is the world's finest science writer and the world's second best science fiction writer." Asimov, Clarke says, reciprocates.

Clarke's vision of the world, however, is always rooted in science fact. His notions, for example, on the future of man's evolution begin by paralleling those of Dr. Clynes, who draws his conclusions on the basis of empirical data gathered in the laboratory. Clarke, too, believes that man will ultimately be superseded by humanlike computer entities. He points to the possibility of programming personalities into computers, after having discarded all bodily parts, including the brain. For a while, he says, there is the possibility of man and superintelligent computers coexisting side by side; but ultimately he believes man will be "phased out" and the computer beings will go on to construct even greater intelligences. "The machines will prevail simply because their potentialities are so much greater."

The evolution of man to computerlike cyborg and beyond pervades the film *2001,* about which a great deal has been written, presumably by way of "interpretation." Unfortunately, the murk seems to gather a little more heavily with each attempt at illumination, particularly since so many want to attribute visions of drug-abetted hallucinogenic salvation to the puzzling conclusion of the film. For better or worse, I have constructed my own exegesis, based on readings of the novel by the same name, on readings of the short story on which the novel and script were based, on my conversation with Clarke and, of course, on repeated viewings of the film. Though the particulars of the following interpretation will only be meaningful to aficionados of the film and/or novel *2001,* the general import of the film should be of interest to all readers of *this* book.

First that strange black "monolith," that eerie slab of something that keeps reappearing throughout the film, seems to represent the presence of a superintelligence that is keeping earth under surveillance. This is a superintelligence that begins to find life on the planet interesting at the point when pre-anthropoid beings (the apelike creatures of the opening sequences) discover tools and thus doom themselves to obsolescence. Remember that in the opening chapter of this book that discovery was highlighted as the very thing that gave rise to mankind. "The old idea that man invented tools," Clarke said, "is . . . a misleading half-truth; it would be more accurate to say that *tools invented man.*"

The film leaps from the discovery of those tools at the hand of prehuman creatures to the world of man with a host of new tools, tools capable of carrying him into outer space. Computers have replaced bones—and man, the perceptive viewer immediately gets an inkling, is on the verge of something new, perhaps *his* obsolescence. At any rate, the monolith shows up again—this time buried on the moon—and when man comes into its vicinity it emits a monumental wail. It seems that the buried monolith is in fact a celestial alarm system whose electromagnetism has been preserved over the centuries in superconducting coils deep inside it. The sort of signals that emanate from the system are shortly found to be emanating from yet another source—this one farther out in the solar system. To earth scientists, this is obviously the sophisticated contrivance of extra-terrestrials, an alarm system designed to let them know when life on earth had made the next big leap in its evolution, traveling into space with cybernetic tools. The distant signals lure them even farther into the great abyss—from the moon to the far reaches of the solar system.

It's the computerized Discovery I, an interplanetary spaceship, that is finally launched in pursuit of the mysterious bait laid out by the unseen superintelligence. By this time earth's scientists have surmised something of the nature of the creatures behind that intelligence: "In their explorations," Clarke says of them, "they encountered life in many forms, and watched the workings of evolution on a thousand worlds. They saw how often the first faint sparks of intelligence flickered and died in the cosmic night. And because, in all the galaxy, they had found nothing more precious than Mind, they encouraged its dawning everywhere. They became farmers in the field of stars; they sowed and sometimes they reaped. And sometimes, dispassionately, they weeded."

Trouble erupts on the Discovery I when the talking computer, the Hal 9000 (addressed by his teammates simply as Hal), decides to take over the entire mission himself. He kills all the astronauts aboard, except one —who manages to save himself by giving Hal what amounts to a frontal lobotomy. Still, Hal is the intended hero. "There's no question but Hal's the good guy," Clarke insists. "It's just that he'd been mucked up by his *human* programmers." Presumably when computers are doing their own programming this will no longer be a problem, or at least so great a problem.

At last, then, it's just astronaut Bowman. He alone must push on toward Jupiter in search of the source of those mysterious signals. As he approaches what seems to be his quarry—that monolith again—it expands in size and opens up on top. By this time Clarke is calling it the Star Gate. "David Bowman," the text reads, "had time for just one broken sentence which the waiting men in Mission Control, nine hundred million miles away and eighty minutes in the future, were never to forget: 'The thing's hollow—it goes on forever—and—oh-my-God!—*it's full of stars!*' "

So the star-struck Bowman in his little space pod hurtles down this transdimensional duct perhaps thousands of times faster than the speed of light, time coming to a standstill, masses fluctuating from the infinite to the invisible. Stars streak by in a psychedelic explosion of colors. Then, shooting out the other end of this not so endless tunnel, Bowman sweeps out over an eerie landscape where everything gives the impression of being in the photographic negative, symbolizing another dimension of space and time. Bowman sees other tunnels and notices objects shooting in and out of them. "In a flash of insight that might have been wholly spurious, he knew what this thing must surely be," Clarke writes. "It was some kind of cosmic switching device, routing the traffic of the stars through unimaginable dimensions of space and time. He was passing through a Grand Central Station of the galaxy."

Soon the astronaut finds himself hurtling down yet another of these far-out booby hatches, "falling between infinite ebon walls, toward another distant patch of stars." When he comes out it is into a world of space similar to that with which he is familiar, but gigamiles from earth. Here he sees all the exotica of astronomy at relatively close range: red stars, white dwarfs, globular cluster.

As Bowman drifts toward one of the huge red suns he reflects that he has "been caught in an ancient, automatic trap, set for some unknown purpose, and still operating when its makers had long since passed away. It had swept him across the galaxy and dumped him (with how many others?) in this celestial Sargasso, doomed soon to die when his air was exhausted."

But then logic reasserts itself as it dawns on him that he has been protected by those "makers," for he has survived the immense radiation of the sun he is approaching and has lived through incredible accelerations (the "energies of the stars raced past him, as if they were in another universe"). Bowman, boggled by all of this, simply awaits "whatever has been prepared."

Suddenly he finds his space pod settling down on a hard surface in silence and night. The light returns and *voilà*—Bowman thinks he must be mad, for the pod is resting on the polished floor of an elegant hotel suite. Bowman gets out, after recovering from his initial shock, and examines his surroundings. There is a telephone book labeled Washington, D.C., which provides him with "objective proof that, although all this might be real, he was not on earth": the book is a phony. The "Washington" has been copied from a newspaper photograph and the pages—made of a patent imitation of paper—are all blank. Nearly everything in the suite is fake—books, magazines, etc., apparently intended not to deceive, however, but to reassure, to provide familiar surroundings.

Bowman, who thinks he might be undergoing some kind of intelligence test, yields to the situation, eats some of the strange food his "hosts" have left for him; the food at least is real. He finds, too, that the television is real, transmitting all the conventional earthside westerns and headache remedies. Curiously, though, all the programs are about two years old and so are the dates on the magazines. Bowman realizes immediately that it was two years before that the lunar monolith was discovered and reasons that it was then that preparations for his arrival were made. Suddenly the very suite he is occupying flashes across the screen; in it is a celebrated actor denouncing his unfaithful mistress, proof that "his hosts had based their ideas of terrestrial living upon TV programs they began monitoring after the 'alarm' went off."

Bowman, for lack of anything else to do, crawls into bed and goes to sleep. In his slumber, the destiny that has been planned for him begins to take shape. He finds his life unreeling like a tape recorder. Everything, as he sweeps back toward his childhood, is being drained from him. "But nothing was being lost; all that he had ever been, at every moment of his life, was being transferred to safer keeping. Even as one David Bowman ceased to exist, another became immortal. . . . In an empty room, floating amid the fires of a double star twenty thousand light-years from Earth, a baby opened its eyes and began to cry."

Suddenly a monolith, this time crystal, appears before the child, who realizes "that here was the origin of many races besides its own." David Bowman has evolved. The Starchild gazes back at earth, contemplating its future. The man-ape who discovered that he was "master of his world" is going to have to give way to a new master. The magic of the bones, which the man-apes learned could be used as weapons, is being replaced by the magic of a transmuted superintelligence. Full circle.

The encapsulated fetal presence visible at the end of the movie, of course, is merely symbolic of a new evolutionary order, just as the space odyssey itself is symbolic of the evolutionary journey from man to creature of radiation envisioned by Clarke. The astronauts start out to begin with in a large, unwieldy spaceship whose complex functions are viable only in so far as they are computer-directed. Man-computer symbiosis then gives way to something more ethereal, symbolized by Bowman's presence in the tiny space pod that is ejected from the mother ship. In the final stage of evolution, we see Bowman fetalized and translucent, encapsulated in a transparent bubble, at one with the universe.

The parallel here with the evolution of Clarke's unseen extraterrestrials is striking; it is, in fact, the evolutionary destiny he envisions for mankind. First, he says, these extraterrestrials, once ordinary men like ourselves, stored their bodies in computerlike machines, then only their brains, discarding all their natural appendages. Finally they ceased even to exist as machine entities and learned to store knowledge in the "structure of space itself, and to preserve their thoughts for eternity in frozen lattices of light. They became creatures of radiation, free at last from the tyranny of matter." Which brings us to Clarke's Third Law: "Any sufficiently advanced technology is indistinguishable [to man] from magic."

MAN-AMPLIFIERS AND TELEOPERATORS

Utopian as Dr. Clynes' meiotic machines and Clarke's lattices of intelligent light seem, they may not be nearly so remote as one might at first think. A quick look at cyborg development reveals that man's probable successor has come a long way in remarkably short time. Edwin G. Johnsen, chief of the Equipment Branch of the Atomic Energy Commission/NASA Nuclear Propulsion Office just outside Washington, D.C., and William R. Corliss, a physicist, have chronicled the genesis of dozens of man-machine systems in a survey for NASA's Office of Technology Utilization.

"At first we had a hell of a time settling on a name

for these things," Johnsen says, explaining that "cyborg" covers the field but has an ominous ring to it. Numerous proposals got the ax, including such labels as "manipulators," "remote-control devices" and "robots." Manipulators, Johnsen says, is too narrow a concept, since it excludes machines that are actually worn by the human operator, such as powered exoskeletons. Remote control is too broad, including as it does everything that man does at a distance, such as changing a TV channel from his armchair. Robots are preprogrammed automata and are not linked to humans in any way. Finally the two struck on "teleoperator," which they defined as a "general-purpose, dexterous, cybernetic machine." They added that the "man-machine systems that fall through our semantical sieves allow man to: pick up and examine samples of lunar surface while remaining on earth; repair underwater oil pipelines from a surface ship; manipulate radioactive nuclear fuel elements in a hot cell; lift a ton-sized load (the man-amplifier concept); regain dexterity with an artificial limb (the prosthetics concept)" and, as we shall see, much more.

"We went from the concept of a simple master-slave manipulator in a hot cell back in the mid-forties," Johnsen explains, "to systems under development now that will project and amplify man's senses and manipulative capabilities to remote and hostile environments without endangering the man himself." This sort of total man-machine partnership, he adds, "is essential to the large-scale exploitation of space and the oceans."

Engineers at General Electric's Specialty Handling Products Operation in Schenectady, New York, agree. For the past few years they have been developing an extensive line of CAMS (Cybernetic Anthropomorphous Machine Systems), whose qualifications as cyborgs are unimpeachable. One of the first of these was "Handyman," a master-slave system used for handling radioactive materials that consists of two sets of arms. The human half of the system straps himself into the exoskeletal master arms that conform in shape and size to the other, remote set of slave arms. In this harness, the human operator enjoys a sense of spatial correspondence and force feedback that permits him to control the "slaved" mechanical arms remotely, through electronic links, as if they were actual extensions of his own body. Spatial correspondence causes the slaved arms to mimic every motion of the master arms. And force feedback, transmitted through sensors in the mechanical hands and detected in force reflectors in the control harness, allows the operator to "feel" objects being picked up or touched, thus enabling him to gauge and control the amount of force necessary for each task.

Once Handyman and other master-slaves had demonstrated the feasibility of hand-arm teleoperators, researchers naturally began experimenting with leg-foot systems as well. The work was spurred on by the U. S. Army's request for a feasibility model of a CAM quadruped capable of carrying 500 pounds through rough, off-road terrain with the agility of a mountain goat, or something approaching it. In 1969 the result of the million-dollar project was fueled up with gas and "loaded" with its human component—GE's Ralph S. Mosher, a mechanical engineer who has been pioneering in the cyborg field for fifteen years—and taken through its paces. At first glance the Walking Truck, as this particular CAM is called, looks like a four-legged robot, a gleaming metal monster that stands eleven feet high and weighs nearly 3000 pounds. It moves about on its hydraulic haunches with surprising fluidity and grace, suggesting a well-trained circus elephant. Mosher, tucked within the beast's entrails, is more than a passenger; he is its brain and nervous system.

Strapped inside a control harness, electronically and hydraulically linked to the machine's appendages and equipped with sophisticated force reflectors and actuators, he has only to go through a simple crawling motion to make the quadruped move along, amplifying and extending his every movement. With the flick of a wrist he can toss 175-pound railroad ties out of his path as if they were toothpicks; by slamming his foot down he can produce a 1500-pound wallop via the

162

machine's corresponding hind leg. As Mosher puts it, "the man-machine relationship is so close that the experienced operator begins to feel as if those mechanical legs are his own; you imagine that you are actually crawling along the ground on all fours—but with incredible new strength."

Now GE, under the direction of Walter E. Gray, manager of all the CAM projects, is setting out to build a two-legged pedipulator, capable of taking giant strides across the countryside. They have already demonstrated the feasibility of an eighteen-foot pedipulator (which, like the Walking Truck, has a man in it). "Actually," Gray says, "the two-legged version ought to be far easier to learn to operate, simply because it is more anthropomorphic. I see no reason why we couldn't build one capable of swinging through the trees, climbing hand over hand, getting down on all fours when necessary—one that could get around just like an ape or a monkey."

Mosher and Gray foresee the development of both mini and maxi versions of the pedipulator in the near future. "The Institute of Defense Analyses," Mosher says, "is very interested in the mini model." This one —which may be only a couple feet high or even smaller—is expected to come equipped with a small television "eye" and would be operated remotely by a man in a full-size control harness. The Institute, Mosher speculates, probably has reconnaissance, surveillance and possibly sabotage missions in mind for the manipulator. "This little devil," he says, "ought to be able to take care of itself far better than an ordinary man" and if it gets caught its "better half" won't. In addition, its master will know when it gets caught and will be able to punch a destruct button, letting the slave serve double duty as a personnel mine.

As for the maxipulator, Gray believes that pedipulators with fifty-foot legs are not out of the question. When I asked what such a colossus would be used for, Richard Blackmer, manager of GE's Advanced Engineering Division, irreverently quipped that it "might come in handy in forty-nine-foot water." The fact is, Gray says, it *would* be quite a wader and, of course, could also step over some pretty impressive obstacles. Moreover, its giant strides might come in handy on the vast expanses of the moon, on other planets and even on the battlefield.

"TELEFACTORING": A NEW WAY TO TRAVEL

Among the most impressive of GE's many CAM projects is ARMS, a triple acronym dreamed up by Blackmer, the space expert who directed development of the fuel cells and related electrical controls for Project Gemini. What ARMS amounts to is a space repairman, an orbiting, remotely controlled CAM that will be permanently on call, ready to carry out repair, rescue and refurbishment missions in a community of synchronous satellites, manned space stations and transient space craft. The first phase of the project—the study phase—was called Application of Remote Manipulators in Space. The second phase, Blackmer says, "involves development of the first prototype hardware and is called the Anthropomorphous Remote Manipulator System." This is the current stage. The final, fully operational phase—perhaps only four or five years away—will be called Android on Remote Maneuvering Satellite. Funding is being shared by the Air Force's Aero Propulsion Laboratory and NASA.

As the scenario reads now, numerous CAM repairmen will orbit the earth, receiving and carrying out orders from ground control stations. Orbited by boosters such as the Titan 30, the ARMS systems will navigate on command, using directional thrusters, to rendezvous and dock with the satellite or craft in need of repairs. "Dead arms" will be used to grasp the "patient" while two intricately articulated arms and hands, which will correspond precisely to the arms and hands of a human operator on earth, will be used for the actual repair work. Television eyes located on the CAM head, which will project up out of its boxlike body, will provide the human part of the system with a stereoscopic view of the operation. In addition to this visual feedback, the earth operator will also experience force feedback so that he can feel the various components that he will be removing or repairing across 22,000 miles.

Apart from replacing batteries, exchanging tape components and experimental packages, repairing small parts that can knock out an entire satellite and so on, ARMS is expected to update a number of satellites, thus reducing the costs of early obsolescence. If there are at least 130 satellites in synchronous (geostationary) orbit by 1980, as expected, savings from these operations could be considerable. GE and NASA studies indicate that seven repair jobs will more than pay for each ARMS system (which, incidentally, will be largely self-servicing). If used for astronaut rescue missions, for exploration, for in-space construction jobs or for destruction or disarming of hostile satellites, their value will be enhanced immeasurably.

Blackmer, who says he hopes to see test models flown in the early 1970s, observes that "there are no hardware obstacles in our way. We have the means at hand right now to build these things." With that in mind, it shouldn't be too difficult to imagine far more advanced space cyborgs for the near future. William E. Bradley, an engineering authority on electronics and solid-state physics and an assistant vice-president for the Institutes of Defense Analyses "think tank" in Arlington, Virginia, has coined the word "telefactoring," which he defines quite simply as "doing something at a distance." The telefactors Bradley has in mind, however, would not only perform repairs in space but explore it as well, replacing man physically but not mentally in this hazardous undertaking.

Johnsen of the Space Nuclear Propulsion Office has begun drumming up support for Bradley's concept, constantly enlarging on its possibilities. They envision telefactors that would be "slaved" in every conceivable way. Astronauts, or in this case terranauts, strapped into control harnesses on earth, could, in the Bradley-Johnsen visualization, roam through space, walk the surface of the moon, the asteroids or even Mars without "lifting off" as much as an inch. Linked by radio and television and by audio-visual, tactile force and perhaps even olfactory and gustatory feedback to their mechanical slave doubles, they would miss nothing of the actual space experience and at the same time would risk nothing either. And, thanks to the superstrength of their mechanical proxies, they would maneuver through space and across the distant planets without weighty and expensive life-support systems.

Most of the technology necessary for telefactoring is at hand. Tactile feedback systems are still in their infancy, but promising work is under way at Stanford University's Research Institute. Scientists there recently developed fingertip-size air-jet stimulators that may be the forerunners of sophisticated tactile systems that will extend our ability to distinguish even between the textures of silk and velvet over hundreds of thousands and perhaps even millions of miles. Force feedback already lets man determine the presence and shape of objects and to some extent their relative hardness over great distances. Head-controlled television systems providing sophisticated visual feedback have been developed by Philco and other companies and are constructed in such a way that the slave's "eyes" always look in exactly the same direction as the master's.

This leaves only the time-lag problem, in cases where master and slave are separated by millions of miles. For example, signals traveling at the speed of light (186,000 miles per second) will still take nearly three minutes to get back to earth from a telefactor on Mars, making for some serious coordination problems. In some instances, of course, this problem can be overcome simply by putting the master in an orbiting space craft or space station. In others, where operation from earth is necessary or desirable, Johnsen believes that move-and-wait tactics and "predictor controls" will come to the rescue. On the basis of known environmental factors, predictor devices can construct computer models that will look ahead in time and actuate appropriate feedback. Stanford, General Motors and others are at work on such controls.

Confident that the time-lag problem will be overcome, Johnsen creates this word picture to dramatize the art of telefactoring or teleoperating: "Imagine a man wearing a lightweight exoskeleton to control the arms, legs and torso of a distant teleoperator and a head-controlled system (looking something like a motorcycle helmet) to control the teleoperator's television camera. The man receives back through the exoskeleton visual, audio, motion and force feedback. Microminiaturized air-jet transducers under his fingertips pick up and convey the tactile information. Now, by providing any number of duplicate exoskeletons, scientists, engineers, doctors and even the average person can vicariously participate in scientific experiments and remote exploration. Imagine, for example, 'feely TV' with thousands of remote-console receivers with people wired into them, all getting the feel of digging on the moon or Mars and seeing the actual scene—while only one operator, the astronaut, is actually in the control loop, either here on earth or in orbit."

Johnsen and others believe that teleoperators of this sort will be used for terrestrial operations as well: in disaster areas, in mining, in nuclear facilities, in warehouses, in medicine. Doctors at Boston General Hospital, Johnsen points out, are taking very seriously the notion of telediagnosis (see Chapter Two). So far this amounts only to examining patients over closed-circuit television systems that link the hospital with the Boston airport. "But there's no reason why manipulators couldn't be attached to the television," Johnsen says, "so that the doctor could actually thump the patient on the chest, look into his ear, take his pulse and so on, all without leaving his office or wasting precious time on the road. With the advent of precision feedback, telesurgery is likely to become a reality, permitting surgeons from all over the world to plug into the system and form a team without leaving their respective countries."

DISEMBODIED BRAINS

Applications for this breed of sophisticated cyborgs of this variety are as far-ranging as the human imagination. Ultimately, it has been suggested, machines may be made to respond to the spoken word (as we have seen, computers that do just this exist now, though as yet on a limited scale), the slightest gesture, even to thoughts, which, after all, have very precise electrical potentials that can be tapped and channeled, thus making ever more cozy the symbiosis that is quickly developing between man and machine. There are experimental automobile braking systems that can be activated by merely lifting an eyebrow, cutting, in the process, the reaction time required by a foot-brake system by more than 50 per cent. How much longer will it be until equally quick and unobtrusive physiological mechanisms control acceleration, starting and so on, until man *becomes* the machine?

Amputees now have at their disposal artificial limbs that are actuated by thought. Developed by researchers at Harvard and the Massachusetts Institute of Technology, motors in the artificial arm pick up electrical signals from the brain so that when the amputee wishes to raise his arm he has only to think about it and up it goes. The military is now experimenting with mounted guns (some in use on helicopters) that are linked to the human eye, following its movements with precision. At the press of a button or very firm flick of the eye, the gun fires at and invariably hits whatever the human eye is focusing on. So much for that old line: "If looks could kill . . ."

One day, some scientists are convinced, human brains will be implanted in computerized mechanical bodies, achieving what has been called "total prosthesis." The proposition that a brain can be sustained in the living state outside the body is supported by the experiments of Dr. Robert J. White of Western Reserve University in Cleveland. Dr. White succeeded in maintaining a number of monkey brains in isolation. And the Russians, according to the RAND Corporation's *Soviet Cybernetics Review,* are experimenting with disembodied cat brains—but with *military* rather than medical motivation. The Soviets apparently hope to link the feline gray matter to artificial maintenance and sensing systems, creating bio-cybernetic guidance packages for implantation in air-to-air missiles! The cybernized cat brains will, if all goes as planned, be able both to recognize optical impulses emanating from their targets and to transmit guidance signals accordingly, so that the missiles always stay on target.

As for putting a human brain into a computerized body, such noted scientists as Dr. James Bonner, a Cal Tech biologist active in genetics, scarcely blinks at the suggestion. When brains become too large through genetic engineering to carry around comfortably, Dr. Bonner says, what is to prevent us from coming up with brains "that will stay in one place and send their sense organs out into the world?" In fact, he adds, there might be spectacular advantages to computerized bodies (beyond the obvious) such as acquisition of entirely new sense organs. Acquisition of an organ for sending and receiving microwave signals, for example, "would be very convenient for communications at a distance," he says.

Other new capabilities might be added without recourse to such radical procedures as total prosthesis. The military, for example, is experimenting with microminiature infrared viewers designed to give the soldier nighttime vision. Someday these may be worn like contact lenses. Some also believe that it will be possible to alter man's sensory equipment electromechanically so that he will also be able to sense temporal and directional changes, rendering obsolete both the watch and the compass. Other "special effects," such as the ability to breathe under water and detect radioactivity, may be built into the new model of man. According to a report in *Nature,* the ability to detect radiation has been bestowed on a group of experimental cats, each of which is wired into a portable, miniature geiger counter that telemeters electrical impulses directly to the feline brain via implanted electrodes. The square-wave electrical pulses are similar to normal nervous impulses. They are transmitted to a portion of the brain that is associated with fear reactions, causing the cats to shy away from radioactive sources.

As for breathing under water like a fish, systems are being developed by which land animals are able to breathe water through their own lungs for substantial periods. Using their lungs as modified gills, mice, for example, have survived for up to twenty-four hours under water. Now a Dutch scientist at the University of Leyden has reported that dogs, too, can survive prolonged periods under water and then readapt to air. Experiments with humans have not yet yielded such dramatic results, but they have begun.

LINKING THE BRAIN TO THE COMPUTER

The most dramatic extension of man's senses will occur when his brain is linked directly to the computer. Computers, after all, are capable of "thinking" approximately one million times as fast as the human brain. Even assuming a typing speed of 200 words a minute, man can transfer only 10 to 30 bits of information per second, while the computer can handle well over 7000 bits per second. And while the brain can commit to long-term memory only one bit of information per second, computers can store more than one million bits per second. Computers with "vocabularies" up in the millions of words, terms and phrases have been in existence for some years.

Getting at the information contained within the computer has long been a stumbling block. The computer's input and output units simply do not operate with the speed and facility of its other two hardware components—the memory unit and the central processor where the calculations take place. Chapter One dealt with a number of new approaches to man-machine communications. But even when some of these are perfected there will still be a great deal to be desired. Oral inputs and outputs, though certain to make man feel more comfortable with his computer colleagues, for example, are not very rapid. What is really needed is some means of putting the brain "on line" with the computer, hooking it up directly to the computer so that there are no peripheral input or output systems whatever, so that communication will be *by thought transference alone.*

Incredible as this prospect seems, experiments at the Air Force Cambridge Research Laboratories, among others, have demonstrated that direct brain-computer communication is feasible. In these experiments Dr. Edmond Dewan has taken advantage of the fact that people can be taught to control *voluntarily* certain aspects of their brain-wave activity (more on this in the final chapter), specifically the so-called *alpha waves,* a rhythmic electrical activity with a frequency of eight to twelve cycles per second. With proper training an individual can be taught to turn alpha on and off at will. The signals are picked up by electrodes that are affixed to the forehead and other portions of the scalp with a special conductive glue and then, after undergoing filtration to remove "noise," are channeled by EEG machine directly to a computer. The individual communing with the computer in this way "thinks" bursts of alpha into the machine in a pattern that conforms with a prearranged type of Morse code. The computer rapidly analyzes the long and the short bursts of alpha and translates them into the appropriate letters, typing them out on a teleprinter as it does so. Though crude, the technique does point to more sophisticated direct-communications systems for the future. With *implanted* brain electrodes (such as those discussed in the next chapter), for example, a far more intimate communications exchange may be possible.

Dr. Grey Walter, head of research at the Burden Neurological Institute in Bristol, England, and a pioneering investigator in the field of physiological aspects of personality and mental illness, uses other brain waves to "command" computers silently. Dr. Walter is the discoverer of the so-called expectancy or E-wave, an electrical potential that arises in the brain about one second before a voluntary action, which can be either a motor act (such as pushing a button) or simply an "action" with respect to making a firm decision about something. Both the E-wave and a similar intention or I-wave can be channeled into computers "through judicious filters and trigger circuits," Dr. Walter says, and "in this way a subject can learn to obtain a desired experience at will, without physical action."

The E- and I-waves can be used to stop and start machines or to make pictures materialize or disappear on a computer-linked television screen. Instead of pushing a button to make one picture disappear and another appear, the individual simply wills these things to happen. Dr. Walter calls this "auto-stop" and "auto-start." The peculiar rise in electrical potential "preceding a voluntary action," he notes, "can be used directly to initiate the computers and stimulus generators. The electronic threshold at which this occurs can be gradually reduced by the experimenter so that, for example, the exposure of pictures [on the TV screen] begins to occur just before the subject has actually pressed his button. This is called 'auto-start.' An intelligent subject soon realizes that his intended action has had the expected result before he has actually moved his finger and usually ceases to bother to press the button: the pictures appear as and when he wants them. . . . For this effect to be sustained it is essential that the subject really 'want' the event to occur and concentrate on evoking this particular event. . . . Auto-start can be combined with auto-stop so that the subject can acquire a picture by willing its appearance on the TV screen and then erase it, as soon as he has completed his inspection of it.

"From the standpoint of the subject, this is a very peculiar experience, sometimes accompanied by signs of suppressed excitement. . . . An intriguing variation is to arrange that the pictures which the subject can acquire are his own intention and expectancy waves relayed by a TV camera focused on the moving (EEG) record. In this situation the 'intention' potential falls more slowly after its initial rise since the subject can watch it from the moment it triggers the exposure and his interest delays its subsidence." Here, then, communication is not only from brain to computer but also from *brain to computer to brain.* Some of the remarkable applications of such communications loops, apart from facilitating man-machine symbiosis, will be examined in detail in the final chapter.

TOWARD "ELECTRONIC NIRVANA"?

Once it is possible to plug directly into the nervous systems with computers and other electronic exotica, the possibilities become almost boundless. Cybernetic man will, as Clarke predicted, then be able to enter into temporary unions with any of a number of machines: "not merely to control, but to *become* a spaceship or a submarine or a TV network." Maurice J. Ponte, a Fellow of the International Institute of Radio Engineers, has already outlined the workings of the television cyborg, a creature that he believes will surface within the next thirty years. The optic nerves, he says, will be "directly excited by electrodes connected to the [TV] receiver." So much for picture tubes.

Not everyone, of course, is delighted by the prospect of "bionic" engineering since it, in effect, renders the present model of man obsolete. Some see in all these heady "advances" nothing but capitulation to machines. It is only fair that these individuals be given their say at this point, and for that purpose I have chosen to quote at length from an entertaining and informed article written by another distinguished Fellow of the Institute of Radio Engineers, Daniel E. Noble, a ranking executive of Motorola, Inc. The article, "Electronic Nirvana," was published in the *Proceedings of the IRE:*

> Today's parents use the TV as a pacifier for temporarily immobilizing children of all ages, but the parent of the future will resort to a much more scientific solution. At birth, the infant will be clamped in

front of the TV eye by means of a suitable supporting structure, and two sections of tubing will be connected to provide nourishment and to carry away the
waste materials. From this time on, the subject will
live an ideal vicarious life, scientifically selected for
compatibility with the fixed influences of the inherited
genes and chromosomes. For the early years, the automatically programmed TV will process the storing
of the necessary bits in the memory brain cells of the
subject for use in the initial "thinking" responses.

As the accumulation of working material in the
memory progresses, the "teaching" will be alternated
with programmed vicarious living experiences. As the
subject grows older, the victim—I mean the subject—
will be trained in the necessary mental processes for
selecting, storing, rejecting, correlating, disciplining,
arranging and re-arranging new combinations of bits
in the memory cells to enhance the potential for this
more advanced thinking capability.

It is obvious, of course, that various essential sensors will be connected to master points in the subject's nerve-responsive system, and as the intellectual
and emotional patterns emerge, the subject will be
exposed to graded influences which will be selected
automatically and will be totally controlled by the
feedback from these sensors. A permanent recording
of all sensor reactions properly coded to the influ-
encing subject matter will be made for analysis and/
or use later in the continuing programmed activation
of the telememory transducers which will directly
stimulate a selected retrieval from the memory brain
cells. As a result of the transducer stimulation, the
subject will relive past vicarious experiences without
recourse to sight or sound.

Other transducers, properly controlled by the sensors, will be used to create and store additional sensations associated with the senses of touch, smell and
taste. A library of qualified selections of vicarious liv-

ing experiences will accumulate in solid-state memory form and will be automatically selected by the coded sensors for maintaining the "happy" state of the subject.

In time, the memory cells of the subject will become saturated, or at least will be supplied to an adequate level with vicarious living experiences so that listening and viewing the TV eye will no longer be necessary. From this point on, the sensors will automatically select the "living" experience which is to be *relived,* and the coded memory transducer will provide the controlled brain stimulus which will release the stored memory for the "reliving" of the vicarious living experience. In this way, the subject will be maintained in a perpetual state of static, innocuous bliss.

As the practice of "electronic nirvana" becomes universal, the natural result will be race suicide. Before this happens, the development of machines which will reproduce themselves will have been completed, and the machines, drawing their raw materials from the ocean, will continue the redundant pattern of automatic machine reproduction and the recreation of simulated human living experiences until finally all of the human subjects will leave the infinity of innocuous existence for the infinity of nonexistence. And so, dear friends, as the sun sets slowly in the east, we leave the beautiful earth with its millennium of technological achievement, with no strife, no mess, and no men, while the machines continue to grind out their fruitless pattern of human vicarious living with no humans present to respond to the stimuli.

A more hopeful outlook is broadcast by Dr. N. S. Sutherland, the computer expert who believes, nonetheless, that within fifty years we will be arguing over whether computers should be entitled to the vote. "A further possibility," he says, "is that we may create a system in which the human brain is linked directly to machine information-processing systems, thus bypassing the slow rate of information transfer through the senses. Stored information on a machine would be available to us as the brain itself requested it internally through, say, a battery of implanted electrodes, and the results of menial calculations could again be made directly available on demand, *thus freeing our own brains for the more imaginative types of thinking.*"

The difference of opinion expressed here points up again the fact that technological "progress" is a complex and highly relative matter; indeed, whether a technological development is progression or regression depends largely upon who (or what) you are at any given moment. Possibly, however, Dr. Noble is being a little unfair to the machines. The "redundant pattern of machine reproduction," for example, is no more to be abhorred than the redundant pattern of human reproduction—now in full swing. What's more, I believe he gives the human species more credit than it deserves when he suggests that man will ultimately get fed up, pull the plug on his electronic synthesizers and opt right out of existence. On the contrary, I think that man, who has demonstrated remarkable fortitude in tolerating (and, truth to tell, in embracing) the banality of television, will literally *thrive* on its successor, electronic nirvana, which, even as outlined by Dr. Noble, provides a multitude of improvements.

If anyone finally tires of the "innocuous bliss" of electronic nirvana, it is liable to be that new breed of intelligent, self-replicating computers. If anybody pulls the plug on man, it is likely to be the machines, not men.

FOUR

MECHANIZING THE MIND

BRAVE NEW WORLD OF ESB

Animals with implanted electrodes in their brains have been made to perform a variety of responses with predictable reliability as if they were electronic toys under human control.
> —Dr. José M. R. Delgado
> Yale University School of Medicine

The once-human being thus controlled would be the cheapest of machines to create and operate.
> —Curtiss R. Schafer
> Electrical Engineer

In the field of brain physiology, I think it [ESB] is the most exciting single discovery. . . . I am almost frightened to say what I think might come of this. . . .
> —Dr. Robert H. Felix
> Testifying before the Senate
> Appropriations Subcommittee on
> Health

Man is possessed of an almost overwhelming desire —some insist that it is actually an *instinct*—to explore, to pit himself against the unknown, to charge headlong into the frontier, whatever its nature, whenever and wherever it might present itself. Alas, the opportunities for challenge, confrontation and conquest on the land inevitably must dwindle as rapidly as the wilderness itself, and that has been very rapidly indeed. Man has blazed his destructive trail to every corner of the earth. DDT is now detectable in significant quantities in the "remote" polar caps; once beautiful lakes and rivers are now open sewers; beer cans and even rusting auto bodies are there at trail's end to greet the most ambitious "wilderness" backpacker; "camping out" is now an exercise in togetherness with no greater challenge than finding a place to park the old (TV-equipped) Kamp King.

Where are the new frontiers? The oceans? Possibly —but only for a few, and for only a little while. Some ecologists fear that even these great bodies of water will be almost irretrievably polluted in two or three decades. Thor Heyerdahl, on his papyrus-borne odyssey across the Pacific, expressed horror at the abundant bobbing, floating, reeking evidence of man's "progress" that persisted even into mid-ocean: cans, bottles, garbage, unidentifiable sludge and, of course, the innumerable and practically immortal oil slicks. More subtly offensive are the tons of pesticides and phosphates that ultimately seep into the oceans from the ground water, not to mention the nerve gas that is deposited there directly by man.

And so, perhaps, space? A good bet, provided we still have enough resources to spend much time there. But even then only a few will ever be able to venture to the other planets (at least in the foreseeable future), though many others may benefit vicariously, as outlined in the preceding chapter. Are there no other possibilities? Yes—*one*. And it could prove to be the most significant wilderness of all, a frontier which, if "conquered," could obviate the "need" for *all* other frontiers. This is the frontier called "mind"; some of the pioneering excursions into this (until recently) almost entirely uncharted world are described in this and the subsequent chapter.

Exploratory progress in this realm has been such to date that Dr. Carl R. Rogers, professor of psychology at the University of Wisconsin, has been moved to state that "we have in the making . . . a science of enormous potential importance, an instrumentality whose social power will make atomic energy seem feeble by comparison." Dr. B. F. Skinner takes a similar view: "Science," he says, "is steadily increasing our power to influence, change, mold—in a word, *control* —human behavior." So does Dr. Robert S. Morison of the Rockefeller Foundation: "Knowledge of human behavior," he observes, "is becoming organized and accumulative. . . . It is becoming scientific. . . . It is not too early to prepare ourselves for the day when there will be a behavioral science which will make possible the control of human behavior with a high degree of precision.

That day, in fact, appears to be dawning. What man will make of it remains to be seen. This frontier, more than any other, has a potential for exploitation by the self-serving and the shortsighted. If wisely managed, however, it can provide the greatest return of all, something that is often yearned for but seldom attained:

peace of mind, possibly even mind leached of its destructive urges.

ELECTRONIC STIMULATION OF THE BRAIN

Though the "battle for men's minds" is being waged on several fronts, attention here is focused on the approach that promises the most dramatic results: electronic stimulation of the brain. ESB, as it is called, provides a means of "mapping" the mind, of locating within the brain the specific sites at which various categories of emotion, feeling, action and thought originate. More than this, ESB provides a means of exerting some *control* over those feelings and actions. It can even help reactivate parts of the brain that have ceased functioning because of disease or trauma, induce immense pleasure, override "intractable" pain and, for a finite period, enable one to relive one's past, even the most remote, "unremembered" past.

Recent rapid development in ESB technique follows upon what was rather a slow start. Direct electrical stimulation of the brain, in fact, dates back nearly two centuries to the experiments of Volta, Galvani, Du Bois-Reymond and others, who discovered that the brain is more susceptible to electronics than to obscure chemical forces ("animal spirits," they were called) that were in vogue up to that time. During the Franco-Prussian War of 1870, battlefield brain surgeons used crude electronic probes that would curl the hair of today's neurologists in an attempt to locate damaged brain tissue. They would simply stick wires into the brain, apply the electrical voltage and wait for some response, a twitch here, a kick there, an erection, excessive salivation, etc.; if *no* response was forthcoming, the surgeon would assume brain damage in the area under stimulation. Then he would generally take scalpel in hand and excise the affected tissue—usually to rather horrible effect.

This medical "technology" lay mercifully dormant for

decades after the war—until Dr. Walter R. Hess, a brilliant Swiss neurophysiologist, devised the modern technique of electrode implantation in 1932, demonstrating in the process that nearly all of man's functions and emotions can be influenced by electrical stimulation of specific cerebral areas. "For the first time," observes Dr. José M. R. Delgado, one of the foremost practitioners of ESB research, "it was revealed that psychological manifestations like rage do not depend exclusively on sensory inputs and physiological stimuli, but can be induced by electrical currents applied directly to the brain. Although these findings did not produce a significant impact on philosophical thinking, in retrospect they may be considered as important as the nineteenth-century demonstration that the contraction of a frog muscle did not depend on circulating spirits and could be controlled by physical instrumentation."

Epoch-making as Hess's work was, it wasn't until nearly twenty years later that he received the Nobel Prize for his discoveries. And it is only now that ESB is coming into its own as a routine procedure in animal studies and, on a much smaller scale as yet, as a clinical tool for treatment of human disorders. As a research tool alone, it is invaluable, for it makes possible, *for the first time,* physiological exploration of the *conscious* mind.

Presenting the annual James Arthur lecture on "The Evolution of the Human Brain" in 1965, Dr. Delgado, a professor of physiology at the Yale University School of Medicine, cautioned that ESB is not a panacea for all of man's woes, "but I do believe," he declared, "that an understanding of the biological bases of social and antisocial behavior and of mental activities, which for the first time in history can now be explored in the conscious brain, may be of decisive importance in the search for intelligent solutions to some of our present anxieties, frustrations and conflicts. Also, it is essential to introduce a balance into the future development of the human brain, and I think that we now have the means to investigate and to influence our own intellect."

WIRING THE BRAIN

To understand fully the impact ESB may have in the very near future, it is important first to understand something of the actual technique of implanting electrodes in the brain. Thousands of laboratory animals, including cats, rats, dogs, dolphins, bulls and even crickets, have been wired, some with more than one hundred electrodes. Dozens of humans, most of them suffering from serious diseases or mental disorders, have been similarly wired—some with scores of electrodes and for periods in excess of a year. To date, electrodes have been left intact in lab animals for more than five years without any visible ill effects.

The procedure for implanting electrodes in humans (basically the same as for animals) goes like this: air or radiopaque material is injected into the intracerebral spaces inside the skull so that the various parts of the brain can be visualized by means of X rays. A metallic skullcap—called a stereotaxic machine—is attached to the head with three or four little spikes that penetrate the scalp. Then X rays are taken from various angles. ESB experiments during recent years have provided increasingly detailed maps of the brain, thus making it possible to pinpoint the exact areas they wish to stimulate. They make geometrical calculations, using the X rays and the reference-point grids of the stereotaxic apparatus, to get three-dimensional coordinates for positioning of electrodes.

When the desired target is fixed, the subject is further anesthetized and small burr holes are drilled into his skull at the appropriate points. Micromanipulators on the stereotaxic machine are used to guide the hairlike stainless steel electrodes through the holes, sinking them to the desired depth in the brain. Some of these electrodes are only a millionth of an inch in diameter —*small enough to be placed inside an individual nerve cell*. Even the larger electrodes, however, leave brain function unimpaired and are entirely painless because the brain itself has no sense of "feel." Once the electrodes are in place, their exposed ends are attached to small terminal sockets that are cemented to the scalp. Electrical current, measured in milliamps in most cases and lasting only fractions of a second, is passed through the sockets and discharged at the tips of the electrodes, providing the desired stimulation of the brain.

Originally, the electrical wires feeding into the sockets were connected to bulky consoles that were immobile for all practical purposes. This had obvious disadvantages since it didn't permit spontaneous movement and, of course, restricted the subject to a small area. Deranged individuals and rambunctious lab animals, moreover, often tried to rip the electrodes out of their skulls with less than felicitous results. To circumvent these serious problems and achieve a more natural man-machine symbiosis, technicians developed stimulators packaged in collars, small backpacks and little boxes that fit securely on the crown of the head. These contain batteries, transistors and timing devices to regulate and control the stimulation. They also serve as receivers, tuned to pick up radio signals from remote operators who can regulate the tempo and intensity of stimulation in whatever way they desire at any given moment.

Researchers at the Yerkes Primate Center in Atlanta have developed a head unit that is even equipped with a solar cell so that free-swinging monkeys need never come in for a recharge. Emphasis is very much on miniaturization, and Yale's Dr. Delgado and his colleagues have developed portable instruments tiny enough to fit inside the head bandages of their human patients. Some of them conceal their electronic headgear under wigs and hats. Very soon researchers hope to have terminal devices that can be wholly implanted under the scalp. But whatever the gear, the result is much the same. When current is discharged into the brain, the patient reacts. He may be induced, for example, to hold his arm out rigidly in front of him. He may be induced to sleep or to work happily. In many cases the patient forgets that he is being artificially stimulated. At any rate he never feels that he is doing something against his own will. Stimulated to make a specific motor action, he "feels" that he himself created the stimulation.

GOVERNMENT BY "ELECTROLIGARCHY"

The incredible power that one can exert over an individual's actions and emotions with ESB has given rise to some alarm. What works for lower animals in this realm can also be made to work for man. Most scientists assume, of course, that this technology will remain in (their) benign hands, ushering in a new era of "electronic nirvana." But if the technology should fall into decidedly unscrupulous hands (and this must certainly be considered a possibility), then a strange and fearful world could result.

An electrical engineer named Curtiss R. Schafer alluded to this very possibility in a paper he presented before the National Electronics Conference in Chicago some years ago. Half in jest, he proposed that computer-controlled electrodes be implanted in the brains of babies a few months after birth, robotizing them for life. "The once human being thus controlled would be the cheapest of machines to create and operate," he pointed out. "The cost of building even a simple robot, like the Westinghouse mechanical man, is probably ten times that of bearing and raising a child to the age of sixteen." Other scientists have admitted the possibility that governments could try to control citizen behavior by techniques of ESB.

The vision of a society controlled by such a government is not pleasant to contemplate—yet it is certainly as "realistic" as that envisioned by Aldous Huxley in his famous novel *Brave New World,* in which the masses were *bio-chemically* stratified via the sort of genetic engineering that is already becoming possible in laboratories around the world. An electronically contrived Brave New World, however, might actually be easier to achieve. The stratification here, of course, would be somewhat different, as the following scenario will demonstrate:

To begin with, let us imagine a conspiracy participated in by a small group of powerful men who seek to "optimize" society. Noting the fantastic potential of ESB, they envision themselves at the top of an electronically sustained socio-structure that might be called the Electrohierarchy. The conspirators, let us say, are leading figures in the military-industrial complex who want to run society in the same way that they run their factories and armies. But now, instead of having to worry about personnel incentive programs, waste, time-consuming interoffice bickering, in-house pilfering and philandering, insubordination, the costly ritual of hiring and firing and so on, they need only punch buttons and transmit the appropriate signals to achieve every general's, manager's, president's, premier's dream of the efficient society. These Electroligarchs might comprise, say, forty or fifty individuals whose brains would remain entirely untouched. On their orders, however, everyone else would have varying numbers of electrodes implanted in his or her skull.

The Electrons, the second rank in such a society, might comprise 10 per cent of the population with fifty implanted electrodes each. Remotely programmed and controlled by the Electroligarchy, they would exhibit unswerving allegiance to their "masters." The Electrons, however, would be society's most creative components. The Electroligarchy would be clever enough, in a corporate way, to give the Electrons their heads—at least to the extent that they could still come up with innovations and discoveries with which to enrich society, such as it would be. The Electrons would be drawn from the society's reserve of scientists, economists, scholars, poets and other "thinkers." They would not be so controlled that they could no longer experience unhappiness or some of the other emotions that often goad individuals on to do creative things. But their potential for hostility and rebellion would be considerably attenuated. And, of course, like all the members of the Electrohierarchy, they would be programmed to "forget" that that had been partially robotized.

Positrons might occupy the next rung down the ladder, possibly comprising 30 per cent of the population. Each would possess some two hundred embedded electrons. These individuals would make up the white-collar support contingent. The Positrons would help put the theories, plans and projects of the Electrons into practice. They would be less imaginative and less intelligent than the Electrons, hence more closely controlled and regimented. They would be characterized by dedication, driven by the desire to implement the goals set by the Electrons. Emotionally, they would be wholly positive thinkers, enthusiastic components of the machine; the more they accomplished, the more pleasure they would receive electronically. They would possess none of the Electrons' negativism, but they would maintain minimal personalities, if only to make them more palatable to the Electrons with whom they would have to make frequent contact.

At the lowest level might come the Neutrons, 60 per cent of the population with five hundred electrons each. These would be the blue-collar people, the factory workers, the soldiers, secretaries, bus drivers, all those engaged in repetitive, often menial tasks. They would be cheaper and more reliable than automatic equipment and mechanical robots. They would, in fact, be completely robotized so that they could dig ditches all day and love every minute of it, if need be.

Even assuming that a centralized computer of sufficient complexity and sophistication to effect such a system is possible, *implementation* would still remain a major obstacle. It would almost certainly be a mistake, however, to assume automatically that it would be *impossible* to implant electrodes in everyone's brain. It might be relatively easy provided people could be persuaded to undergo implantation *voluntarily*. In a world rapidly growing accustomed to artificial external and internal prostheses, spare-part surgery and organ transplants, the idea of implanting metal wires in the brain is bound to become less and less "foreign" and

repugnant. And to push the campaign along, our Electrocrats might offer a number of incentives, perhaps
tax deductions or even cash "rewards." Possibly the
implant program could be ballyhooed into a matter of
"national security," so that refusal to participate would
call one's patriotism into question. Instantaneous communications and electronically augmented "will to resist
the enemy" could be some of the selling points.

More likely, however, is the possibility that people
will opt for the implants in order to "cash in" on a
new form of electronic entertainment. As we shall
see later in this chapter, the so-called "pleasure centers"
of the brain can be wired in such a way that one can
create, with the mere push of a button, an almost
orgasmic state of euphoria or cause the individual to
hallucinate as vividly as if on LSD. With computer
programming it may be possible to create within the
mind synthetic experiences of almost any description.
In addition, it may prove possible to transmit electronically coded information directly into the brain
via the implanted electrodes, creating a radical new
approach to education.

Dorman D. Israel, a Fellow of the Institute of Radio
Engineers, for example, predicts that brain implants
will be much sought after around the turn of the
century to implement new means of communication
(direct electronic thought transference) and enhance
creative capabilities. Writing in the *Proceedings of the
IRE* as if from the perspective of the year 2012, Dr.
Israel notes that by the year 2000 people will be able
to transmit their thoughts over substantial distances
"but always by appointment—a most fortunate limita-
tion." By 2012, he goes on, things will have advanced
to the point that "newborn infants can be operated
upon and the latest submicroelectronic equipment installed in the brain and at certain critical points in the
spinal column so that they are almost certainly assured
not only of the benefits of full nonradio communicative
powers but also there is reason to believe that their
scientific creative ability will be enhanced. Logically
enough, this operation must be performed within two

weeks of birth because if the infant is only slightly exposed to contacts with its family who still have not completed their 'unlearning' and readjustment (to the new technology), he might never become a good subject for the modern system of communication."

Sizable segments of society may already have undergone electrode implantation by the time the "takeover" plot is first hatched. By simply commandeering the by then *existing* computer-coordinated system, the Electrocrats would find that most of their work had already been done for them. When the individual dials into the central computer from his own home requesting, say, pleasurable experience number 547Z, he may then receive instead a carefully contrived series of electronic impulses that instill in him an unswerving loyalty to his unseen masters. Or possibly the stimulation he receives might simply obliterate his will to resist a physical takeover or fill him with a completely debilitating fear of authority. That dramatic behavioral control is possible with ESB and has, in fact, been demonstrated in several laboratories, as we shall see.

ELECTROSLEEP

Like nuclear energy, ESB possesses a fantastic potential for good as well as evil. Having conceded the substantial potential for abuse of this new technology, let us proceed to look at the other, more hopeful side of the coin. In the course of ESB experimentation, scientists have discovered that all of the brain's functions—the automatic, the somatic and the psychic—are susceptible to electrical control. As Dr. Delgado puts it, in "exploring intracerebral physiology, we are reaching not only the soma but also for the psyche itself."

Consider the influence that can now be exerted over the autonomic system which resides largely in the hypothalamus, that deep, dark elemental area of the brain that controls our most basic and primitive needs. It helps regulate blood pressure, heart rate, respiration, hunger, sleep, sex and many other things. Appropriately placed electrodes can alter all of these functions. Cats that have just eaten a large meal can be stimulated to gorge themselves even further, completely ignoring their already distended stomachs. Others, literally starving, can be electronically induced to ignore food placed directly under their noses. The diameter of their pupils can be electrically controlled as if they were the diaphragms of cameras. The doctors can willfully alter the animals' blood pressure and heart rate with precision.

Scientists see many benefits accruing from this sort of control over basic functions. They can, to begin with, get a better understanding of how these functions work and what can go wrong with them, thus arriving at more effective cures for diseases of metabolism, the heart, circulation and so on. Something called "electrosleep," for example, has come to the rescue of numerous human insomniacs, though to date most clinical work has been with external electrodes attached to the scalp. In lab work, however, internal electrodes have been used on animals with encouraging results.

At the Yerkes Primate Center in Atlanta, Dr. Adrian Perachio, a neurophysiologist, is conducting a series of ESB experiments for NASA which may result in a better understanding of what happens to sleep patterns during space travel. Variations in acceleration and gravity seem to affect and perhaps inhibit one critical phase of sleep known as the rapid-eye-movement (REM) phase, during which most of our dreams occur. Humans and lab animals deprived of REM sleep exhibit bizarre and often psychotic behavior; this indicates to some scientists that REM is as essential to life as food and water. Some researchers now claim to be able to stimulate REM sleep at will. This suggests that we may one day be able to cut down substantially on our total sleep time. Why? Because many believe that other sleep phases are merely incidental to the critical REM stage (which constitutes only 24 per cent of healthy sleep time). Thus, if REM could be artificially induced on a routine basis, perhaps through self-stimulation of implanted electrodes at the desired time, one might be able to reduce the period of slumber by 50 to 75 per cent.

On the other hand, it might be useful to *prolong* sleep electronically too. If at the same time heart rate, body temperature and other life functions were slowed down by the proper stimulation of the hypothalamus and other cerebral structures, a state of suspended animation might result, the likes of which could come in handy on extended space journeys. This sort of "hibernation," at any rate, now appears far more feasible than that envisioned by advocates of cryogenic (deep-freezing) suspension.

ELECTROPROSTHESES

Somatic functions have yielded even more dramatically than the autonomic to ESB. These are the motor functions, movements of the body and its extremities, which can be controlled by stimulating various parts of the cerebral cortex. In Dr. Delgado's experiments animals were induced to "move the legs, raise or lower the body, open or close the mouth, walk or lie still, or turn around." He found that the animals took all of this very much in stride, seemingly unaware of the outside interference. Cats stimulated in such a way that they would suddenly have to raise a hind leg would go right on purring. Nor would they stumble or fall. "However," Dr. Delgado observes, "if we tried to prevent the evoked effect by holding the hind leg with our hands, the cat stopped purring, struggled to get free, and shook its leg," indicating that the stimulatory command is a powerful one.

A number of researchers are working to put this sort of motor control to practical effect. Perhaps the most impressive results to date have been achieved by Dr. Lawrence R. Pinneo and his associates at the Stanford Research Institute. Dr. Pinneo is using ESB as an "electroprosthetic" device which he hopes will help paralyzed stroke victims move again. Work is still confined to lab animals but its applicability to humans is apparent. The best thing about electroprosthesis is that it does not require any sort of artificial limb or external attachment. Instead, parts of the brain not damaged by the stroke are stimulated to produce purposeful movements. Computers are used to control the sequence of stimulatory events emanating from as many as sixty electrodes, permitting the animal to move about in a coordinated and almost natural fashion. "With a little training," Dr. Pinneo points out, "the animal can be given a set of switches that tell the computer what set of movements to produce; thus he can enter into control of his own behavior."

For those interested in the specifics of the experimental electroprosthetic technique, Dr. Pinneo and his colleagues (Dr. J. N. Kaplan and E. A. Elpel of the Stanford Research Institute, and P. C. Reynolds and J. H. Glick of the Stanford University School of Medicine) have prepared a paper entitled "Experimental Brain Prostheses: Methods and Possibilities." In it, they write:

This technique involves permanently attaching an electrode guidance platform to the paralyzed monkey's skull while the monkey is anesthetized and in a stereotaxic instrument. The platform is made of dental acrylic and contains an array of holes through which electrodes can be inserted into the brain with stereotaxic accuracy. It is aligned above the monkey's head with the stereotaxic apparatus and is attached to the skull with screws and acrylic dental plastic. The skin below the platform is removed so that electrodes can be inserted directly through the skull without piercing the skin first.

. . . After application of a local anesthetic, a small hole is drilled through the skull using a hole in the platform as a guide. The hole in the skull is made on the side contralateral to the cortical lesion, i.e., on the same side as the paralyzed limb, because most limb movements evoked by stimulation in the brain stem occur on the same side as stimulation. An electrode is lowered into the brain in 1-mm. steps through the hole in the skull. Motor responses to stimulation are initially tested at each step as the electrode is lowered.

After each location is found that produces a distinct elementary motor response, electrodes are permanently fixed by bending the electrode on top of the platform and attaching it to the platform with acrylic. The electrode is then connected to an Amphenol plug that is housed in a box made of acrylic. The box is attached to the guidance platform with screws and is removed from the platform only when electrodes are inserted into the brain. In Bruno (one of the lab monkeys) 13 locations were found that upon stimulation produced movement in his paralyzed right arm. Movements in this limb included rotation of the wrist, arm turning in toward the body from the shoulder, arm straight out from the body, rotation of forearm out from the body at the elbow, flexion of the thumb and several other elementary movements.

The Stanford team uses a LINC-8 digital computer to program and operate the implanted electrodes. The total bio-cybernetic system consists of (1) a ten-channel programmable brain stimulator (more channels are possible for future expansion to accommodate any number of electrodes); (2) the LINC-8 computer with appropriate interfacing equipment; (3) the software programs controlling the system; and (4) the animal itself.

The information needed to produce a given set of movements is encoded, in each case, in a table format called TIMETABLE. Fed into the computer, TIMETABLE specifies the pattern of stimulatory events needed to produce the desired motions. The TIMETABLE repertoire can be altered simply by addressing the computer via teletype. The system also features a magnetic tape input so that TIMETABLE configurations, once proven effective in evoking a specific movement, can be stored for future use and instantaneous retrieval. This is what makes it possible to put together a chain of movements that closely approximates natural, coordinated bodily motion. Complex as the whole system sounds, it has been simplified to the point that, as noted, the monkey can himself operate a small set of switches. With proper training this enables him to control his own movement. He learns, for example, that if he wants to raise his right arm he is to push one switch, if he wants to move rapidly forward he is to push another switch, and so on.

Dr. Pinneo expects to implant as many as 240 electrodes in the brain stem, making possible even more sophisticated cybernetic organisms. He points out, however, that with this much hardware in the brain there is bound to be some significant damage to brain structure. Hence he is now looking for means of achieving deep brain stimulation *without* implanted electrodes, a means that would, in addition, permit stimulation of deep brain sites *without* simultaneous stimulation of *intervening* brain tissue. "In order to stimulate at one point, and one point only and to produce no damage to intervening tissue," he notes, "it is evident that the intensity of the penetrating energy must be below that necessary for tissue stimulation at every point *except* the desired focus of stimulation. This obviously means that two or more sources of energy must be used where each can be focused to a point, and where the point of focus is the site of stimulation. It also means that at the point of focus, the two or more beams of energy must be able to add, in phase, in order to provide a total intensity sufficient to stimulate the tissue at that point." A single energy source sufficient to stimulate the target site, in other words, is no good because it would also be sufficient to stimulate all intervening sites. External stimulators of the future may combine a variety of energy forms, including electric current, electromagnetic radiation (especially at microwave or higher frequencies), ultrasonics and laser beams.

ELECTROVISION

Dr. Pinneo and others, including Dr. Wendell J. S. Krieg, a Northwestern University anatomist, are hopeful that similar electroprosthetic programs can be established for the blind. Though actual experimentation has only begun, Dr. Krieg hopes to help the blind see through the use of light-sensitive photoelectric cells wired directly to the brain. The miniaturized cells, he says, could be worn on the patient's head, perhaps even incorporated into hats. Electrodes feeding out of the cells would be permanently implanted in the portion of the brain that interprets vision.

As a modest start, Dr. Krieg proposes a system capable of detecting and transmitting the shapes of letters so that the blind person would perceive a continuous series of letters and words—in the same manner that the normal person reads the news that is flashed in lights at Times Square. From here, he says, more complex systems could be devised so that pictures resembling animated cartoons could be viewed. Eventually the system could be refined to the point where it would be possible for the subject to perceive variations in light, detect the presence of doors, windows, approaching objects and so on.

"He would be enabled to move more rapidly and safely and to throw away the white cane, which is little more than a tradition or a warning," says Dr. Krieg. He adds that such systems are feasible now since the process for stimulating the visual portion of the cortex is well known. He observes that electrode implants can also be useful in overcoming hearing losses and, like Dr. Pinneo, notes the possibilities for the use of ESB in restoring movement to paralyzed or injured limbs. "It is a comparatively easy matter with a myograph to analyze the exact time sequences of all the muscles of the limbs while walking," he says. "By playing such a record on a stimulator connected to the proper muscles, each muscle could be made to contract at the right time and the result would be normal walking."

Dr. Pinneo and associates have been at work now for more than ten years on an approach to visual prosthesis or "electrovision." So have a number of British researchers, notably G. S. Brindley and W. S. Lewin, who have actually begun working with the human. Brindley and Lewin, in one effort to overcome blindness, implanted eighty platinum electrodes into the brain of a fifty-two-year-old nurse suffering from glaucoma and retinal detachment. The patient was able to "see" a small spot of light, and the British investigators believe that proper programming of the stimulative events will enable the blind to avoid obstacles and possibly read print.

The Stanford team is trying for even better results: "to reproduce normal vision by making the visual system act as it would physiologically with light stimulation of the retina." Dr. Pinneo and his group have now formulated a theory of "brightness" vision and are making headway in their effort to replicate some forms of it electronically. As presently envisioned, the prosthesis system, once perfected, will be much like that for stroke. With computer control, Dr. Pinneo says, "we should be able to present a three-dimensional mosaic of stimulated points representing the entire visual field. . . . For the present, we will only consider black and white representation." Nobody is yet ruling out, however, the possibility of eventually achieving artificial color vision.

The cost and size of computers of sufficient complexity to control these electroprostheses are, at present, considerable. But Dr. Pinneo points to the rapid progress in the miniaturization of electronic componentry as a way around these difficulties. Thanks, in part, to the space program, he thinks we will ultimately have "practical, relatively low cost, general purpose computers small enough to be worn or carried by a human being as part of his clothing."

ELECTROSEX

Intriguing as the electrosomatic devices are, it is the psychic and behavioral functions of the brain that are most spectacularly controlled by ESB. This was demonstrated by Dr. James Olds, who was the first to discover the so-called "pleasure centers" of the brain while experimenting with rats at McGill University in Canada. The nature of the pleasure induced by stimulating these centers (located in a variety of areas) seems to transcend that associated with mere food, drink or sex. The stimulation seems to result in a sort of super-euphoria or hyper-ecstasy that causes the animals to forget more jejune pleasures.

Rats, in one experiment, were "wired for pleasure" and then permitted to press the stimulating lever themselves. And press it they did—some at the astounding rate of 5000 times per hour! Some of these sybarites kept it up for twenty-four hours a day for periods of up to three weeks, taking only the briefest rat naps and scant seconds for food and drink. Conventional sexual intercourse was completely forsaken. "Electrosex," it seems, combines the best of all possible pleasures.

It was discovered, in the course of stimulating human brains to control certain disorders, that man, too, is possessed of these pleasure centers. Dr. Robert G. Heath of Tulane University and Dr. Delgado have both reported this phenomenon in man. Dr. Delgado notes that some patients undergoing stimulation suddenly began discussing sexual matters. Several engaged in flirtatious activity that was out of character with their normal behavior. Most surprising, several of the stimulated subjects expressed their desire to marry the doctor (regardless of whether they were of the opposite sex).

Though the subjects who experienced changes in their sexual ideation apparently experienced pleasurable feelings, they are not necessarily the same, intense feelings that kept the rats up day and night pressing the pleasure pedal. Other human subjects, however, *have* experienced similar pleasures. One man, equipped with one of Dr. Heath's intracranial self-stimulation (ICSS) devices, for example, was particularly fond of pressing one of the buttons on the portable device. According to the reports on this patient, "the feeling [that resulted] was good; it was as if he were building up to a sexual orgasm." Dr. Heath observed that, "regardless of his emotional state and the subject under discussion in the room," the pressing of this particular button "was accompanied by the patient's introduction of a sexual subject, usually with a broad grin. When questioned about this, he would say, 'I don't know why that came to mind—I just happened to think of it.'" The stimulation was a highly effective sexual aphrodisiac and the patient called upon it frequently.

Experiences of possibly even greater intensity have been reported by some of Dr. Delgado's subjects. One woman, while undergoing stimulation of a pleasure center in the brain, found it impossible to control herself. Her mood would abruptly switch from its usual serenity to one of euphoric giggling and laughing. She could only describe what it was that she was feeling as "pleasant tingling sensations of the body." Another patient, who was generally silent, would spontaneously exclaim such things as "Hey! You can keep me here longer when you give me these," when apparent pleasure centers were stimulated.

Just as self-involvement and inward-looking attitudes have been found to characterize many drug-induced "highs," self-orientation seems to accompany the electrically induced pleasure state, at least initially. Some have noted, however, that this preoccupation with internal pleasures gives way with sustained stimulation and pleasurable feelings are expressed, instead, in an increasingly outward direction. Hence, Dr. Delgado says, "a shift from pleasurable thinking to friendliness and to sexual ideas has been observed in some cases."

ELECTROANALGESIA AND ELECTROANESTHESIA

Just as pleasure can be induced by ESB, so can pain be suppressed. "Electroanalgesia," however, generally utilizes the implantation of electrodes in the spinal column rather than in the brain itself. Dr. C. Norman Shealy, chief of neurosurgery at the Gunderson Clinic in La Crosse, Wisconsin, and his colleagues have perfected electroanalgesic techniques to the point that they are now being applied to humans. Electronic painkillers are important because they give strong promise of being useful even in overwhelming the "intractable" pain of incurable cancer and they free the patient suffering any sort of intensive pain from the need to take massive doses of often addicting narcotic analgesics.

Dr. Shealy and his associates have discovered that stimulation of certain areas in the spinal cord can be highly effective in blocking intense pain. Since "intractable" pain has been found to originate in diffuse structures, they selected those areas in the spinal cord where sensory nerve fibers are packed tightly together. This enables them to achieve maximum stimulation with a minimum amount of implanted hardware.

The basic research that preceded clinical application of the electroanalgesic techniques involved cats. They were wired with electrodes and then subjected to varying degrees of pain. "Normally," Dr. Shealy notes, "pinching the tail or paw of the animals leads to meowing and vigorous withdrawal. Similarly, the cats flick an ear to avoid a hot soldering iron. However, when a pulsed D.C. current . . . is applied to a dorsal column electrode over the cervical cord, *the animals allow prolonged pinching and intense heat to the point of tissue damage with no apparent discomfort.* They remain alert during the stimulus and sometimes will sit contentedly licking themselves during the dorsal column stimulation."

Dr. Shealy's first human patient was a seventy-year-old man suffering the severe pain of an inoperable lung cancer. After implantation of a single spinal electrode (with intermittent stimulation at .8 and 1.2 volts), both incisional and original pain were immediately and completely extinguished. This was accomplished, moreover, without paralyzing any part of the patient's body. The patient, Dr. Shealy reports, "maintained good movement of his legs, and vibration, position, touch and pinprick sensations were intact." Pain recurred from time to time but could be immediately obliterated again simply by altering the frequency of the electronic stimulation. At no time did the patient require the accustomed narcotics.

The patient died two days after stimulation was initiated—but for reasons entirely unassociated with the electrode implant. "The initial results were so encouraging," Dr. Shealy reported with regard to this first case, "that it seems reasonable that technical problems can be overcome to make this a potentially practical method for relief of pain."

Since the mid-sixties a number of others have benefited from electroanalgesia, some now for periods measured in years rather than days. Dr. Shealy's second patient, for example, received relief for two years, even though she was suffering from extensive pelvic cancer. His third patient was a fifty-five-year-old man who had been almost completely confined to bed for seven years when seen for treatment. This patient suffered crippling pains in his legs due to infection of a spinal disc. Now he is able to walk and swim freely, thanks to a single tiny electrode implanted in his spinal cord. Whenever he feels a pain developing, he just pushes a button on a miniature transmitter he carries with him and current pulses into the nerve fiber via a tiny receiver implanted beneath the skin. The current "jams" the nerve fibers in much the same way that radio frequencies can be "jammed" to prevent transmission of a message. In this case, however, the "message" that is being intercepted is pain.

Among others wired with self-stimulating units like the one described above are individuals suffering from multiple sclerosis, severe muscle spasms and various carcinomas. Some use the stimulation constantly—so far without ill effect. As before, Dr. Shealy reports, "light touch remains intact as does vibration and position sensation. Patients are able to walk without difficulty. Bladder and bowel function are not affected. Erections and ejaculations are possible during stimulation. The lack of any significant complications in the patients who have been treated . . . should now allow application of this treatment to a large number of patients with chronic pain states."

Electro*anesthesia,* though not so far advanced, may eventually prove to be of equal value. Hundreds die every year from the toxic effects of chemical anesthetic agents; many others suffer severe side effects from their toxic qualities. For most, of course, the chemical anesthetics are neither fatal nor significantly damaging, but they are hard on the system and do take a long time to be eliminated from the body. Electric current, on the other hand, can produce unconsciousness almost instantaneously—without any hangover effect once the operation is complete.

Dr. John Waycott, of the Imperial Chemical Research Laboratory in Great Britain, predicts that electroanesthesia will be a routine hospital technique in the not too distant future. When that day comes a patient requiring general anesthesia will be taken to the operating room fully conscious, wired there with external scalp electrodes and put to sleep with the mere flick of a switch. Once the operation is over, the patient is just as quickly revived, this time by simply turning off the current. Though electroanesthesia has been used many times, a few complications remain to be smoothed out. For one thing, care has to be taken to avoid induction of muscle spasms, a consequence of too much current. In other instances, lungs sometimes cease functioning because of the stimulation and have to be artificially ventilated during the operation. Dr. Waycott, however, is confident that these problems will be overcome with more research into the use of various wave forms and currents and with more precise positioning and use of the external electrodes.

Other notable medical applications of ESB include suppression of epileptic seizure and narcolepsy. Dr. Heath has equipped patients suffering from these maladies with "wireless" self-stimulating transmitters with which they "fire" at will their implanted brain electrodes. When they feel a seizure coming on or (in the case of narcolepsy) feel that they can no longer remain conscious they merely push buttons on their pocket transmitters and thus quickly correct the imbalance in question. Dr. Pinneo is also at work on ESB approaches to problems of consciousness and thinks that even certain forms of mental retardation might be vulnerable to electronic therapy.

"Our approach to both of these deficits is based on the concept of the reticular activating system of the brain stem," he explains, "by which efficient normal behavior is a function of the level of consciousness, or 'arousal.' By electrical stimulation of various areas of the brain, such as the nucleus reticularis, the inferior thalamus and the caudate nucleus, sleeplike states may be produced which in many ways mimic the level of alertness of mentally retarded children or animals. Conversely, electrical stimulation of the mesencephalic reticular formation produces arousal, even in an anesthetized animal, while destruction of this area produces comalike behavior. To date, our experiments using programmed brain stimulation have been minimally successful in controlling level of arousal both upward and downward. It still remains to be seen whether this type of stimulation will affect learning rate in a retarded animal, or return to consciousness an animal suffering from experimental coma."

ELECTROSOCIOLOGY

Violence and affection, like pleasure and pain, are proving susceptible to electronic manipulation. Indeed, even some of the most deep-seated patterns of social interaction can be radically altered with ESB.

Some inkling that ESB might have an "electro-sociological" value came as early as 1928 when the pioneering Dr. Hess discovered that normally gentle cats could be instantaneously driven to states of intense hostility by stimulating certain parts of their brains. The moment the stimulation ceased, so did the hostility. Then in the mid-1950s, Dr. Delgado demonstrated that one animal can be electrically driven to attack another animal—without any ancillary provocation. In one of his first experiments in this area, Dr. Delgado utilized two cats that had always been on friendly terms. The smaller cat was equipped with brain electrodes implanted in a cerebral structure known as the "tectal area." When electrically stimulated, the smaller cat would immediately launch a fierce attack on its larger companion. Even when the large cat began to retaliate with powerful, slashing blows, the small cat persisted. Not until the stimulation was stopped would it withdraw. Normally a cat beaten in battle will go to considerable lengths to avoid the victor. But here the small cat, even though it always lost, fearlessly launched new battles every time it was stimulated in the tectal area of the brain. Initially friendly relations were re-established after each battle, but gradually the larger cat began to regard the other with constant hostility.

Subsequent experiments with cats proved that the sort of rage that is electronically provoked is not an all-pervasive, blind sort of hostility but, as Dr. Delgado puts it, "selective and intelligently directed." Where there were only two cats, the smaller would vent its rage on the other cat, even if it were larger, but if there were a number of cats available it would carefully select as its opponent a less forbidding foe. And, rather than just tear into its target, the stimulated cat would intelligently choose the best moment for attack, approaching the "enemy" with care, adapting its motions to those of the other cat. In other words, brain stimulation of this sort does not obliterate normal patterns of behavioral hostile performance; it "simply" evokes those response patterns where they would not normally exist at all.

The sort of radical societal changes that can be effected by ESB has best been demonstrated in experiments with monkeys, animals that maintain very rigid "rules" with regard to their social interactions. Theirs is a highly autocratic society, in which domains and territories are firmly fixed. In each, the strongest monkey sets himself up as the "boss" or the dictator, reserving for himself first choice of the females, the best food and the most space, while demanding from the others total subservience and submissiveness. Could the boss monkey's well-established dominance be attenuated electronically? And, if so, how would the other monkeys in his group react?

Researchers found that stimulation of various parts of the brain, notably the rostral part of the caudate nucleus, seemed to nullify threatening, dominant behavior. They strapped normally vicious rhesus monkeys into restraining chairs and stimulated this part of their brains. The moment they did so, the monkeys stopped their aggressive behavior. They became so docile that the experimenters were even able to put their fingers in the monkeys' mouths. Hostilities were resumed as soon as the stimulation ceased.

Boss monkeys were then returned to their domains and stimulated by remote control for five seconds every minute. The change in the "dictator" was immediately apparent to the other monkeys, who slowly but surely began moving into territory generally reserved exclusively for the boss. Even after the other monkeys had taken all of his territory, the boss initiated no attacks. In general, he was content to sit back and play a subordinate role. Shortly after stimulation ceased, however, he reasserted his absolute authority.

In one of the most intriguing variations on this experiment, Dr. Delgado again wired one of the boss monkeys so that electronic stimulation could override his normal aggressiveness and authoritarianism. But this time he placed the stimulating lever in the cage with the monkeys. Curious creatures, they naturally began pressing it. After a number of trials they began to notice that they could literally switch off the boss monkey's aggressive behavior simply by pressing the lever—and they did so frequently! Humans might sometimes wish that their own leaders could be controlled as effectively. Indeed, we have here a complete reversal of the situation envisioned earlier in this chapter, in which the autocrats "wire" a subject population in order to "optimize" its productivity. If the power-obsessed minority could be wired *first,* it's conceivable that the majority could get along together in a world free of nuclear brinkmanship, organized military aggression and threats of aggression. *Conceivable.*

Dr. Delgado has demonstrated that even snorting bulls can be "tamed" with the push of a button. In what has to be one of the most flamboyant experiments to date, Dr. Delgado wired a bull with electrodes and, after it had recovered from the surgery, challenged it in the bullring with a red cape. Concealed behind the cape was a small radio transmitter. Dr. Delgado waited until the bull was in full charge and only a couple yards away—then he pushed the button on the transmitter and instantly reduced El Toro to a benign Ferdinand. The bull threw out its front legs and came to a grinding halt just inches from its target.

In still other experiments—these at the Yerkes Primate Center—the meek have been made the aggressors. Three monkeys were placed together: a boss, a female and a subordinate male. As always, the female immediately sided with the boss, completely ignoring the smaller, weaker male. The latter stood meekly by until researchers remotely stimulated an area of its hypothalamus known to excite aggressive behavior. Immediately it sprang into action, advancing on the astonished boss with increasing ferocity. Ultimately it forced the autocrat into a corner and a position of subservience. With an alacrity that must have further humiliated the deposed boss, *the female immediately switched her allegiance to the male she had previously spurned.* "Obviously, this study also showed something about the nature of the female," was the wry observation of one of the Yerkes researchers. Surprisingly, the new boss remained dominant even after stimulation ceased, the old boss having apparently lost face *permanently*. In another of these experiments at Yerkes, the boss was stimulated into a state of rage. One moment he was being groomed in the arms of his beloved; the next moment he was chasing her with murderous rather than amorous intent.

Because of the dramatic results that were obtained in the animal experiments, doctors decided to apply ESB to certain *human* subjects who were given to attacks of unreasoning rage. Some who yielded to the treatment had ten-year histories of rage attacks in which they would assault acquaintances or chance passers-by with deadly weapons and wreck whatever happened to be within easy reach. A team of doctors in Boston has treated a number of such patients at Massachusetts General Hospital and Boston General Hospital. The medical team, consisting of Dr. Vernon Mark, Dr. William Sweet, Dr. Frank Ervin, Dr. George Bach-y-Rita, Dr. Rioji Hagiwara, electrical engineer Gerhard Weiss and Dr. Delgado, describes these cases in the *Journal of Nervous and Mental Diseases:*

1. *L.K.* This 35-year-old male design engineer had . . . frequent episodes of rage during which he assaulted and injured his wife and children. His driving was precarious because he became enraged if other cars cut in front of him and he would go miles out of his way to force them off the road.

2. *M.R.* This 25-year-old male . . . had a police record for vagrancy and violence. He began assaulting his medical attendants on the neurology service of a local veterans' hospital and had to be confined in a mental institution while awaiting surgical evaluation.

3. *J.P.* This 20-year-old female had . . . frequent rage attacks which on more than a dozen occasions resulted in an assault on another person. On one occasion she inserted a knife into a stranger's

myocardium, and another time she inserted scissors into the pleural cavity of a nurse.

4. *G.C.* This 14-year-old girl was brought up in a foster home and was of borderline intelligence. On two separate occasions her violent behavior resulted in the death of a young foster sibling, and she subsequently assaulted a 7-year-old child at the state hospital where she was confined.

Yet another brain-damaged patient, a woman, attacked her husband more than five hundred times in a period of six years, battering him with chairs, dishes and a variety of blunt instruments. Yet even such violent cases proved treatable with ESB, which could often be used to ward off these rage attacks or reverse them completely after their onset on any given occasion.

ELECTROMEMORY AND "THE DREAM MACHINE"

It was in the course of treating brain-damaged individuals that Dr. Wilder Penfield hit upon one of the most astounding properties of ESB. He was probing the brain of a woman with epilepsy at the Montreal Neurological Institute, trying to discover which areas were affected, when he noticed that stimulation in certain regions caused the woman to "relive" various events in her life. At times she thought she was giving birth to one of her children all over again. The detailed accuracy with which this patient, and others on whom Dr. Penfield subsequently operated, recalled experiences, some dating back to early childhood, stunned the surgeon. "No man can, by voluntary effort," he declared, "call this amazing detail back to memory."

Dr. Delgado, who has also observed this phenomenon in a variety of cases, calls what occurs "experiential hallucinations." The electronically induced experiences qualify as hallucinations because, as Dr. Delgado describes them, they often "appear more real and vivid than when the events actually happened. It is as if the patient had a double life, one in the past recalled by the electrical stimulation, and another in the present." The patients not only see and feel things out of their past but even hear and smell them. It has been suggested that "electromemory" may become a valuable tool in psychoanalysis, far outdistancing hypnosis as a means of bringing forgotten experiences to the surface.

The hallucinations are called "experiential" because they usually have some basis in past experience. On some occasions, however, subjects have taken bizarre ESB "trips," experiencing things they couldn't possibly have lived through in the past. This, coupled with the fact that it is possible to stimulate selected parts of the brain sequentially to create various states of mind, suggests that artificial experience might eventually become available to the consumer. It is possible to visualize "dream machines" that would replace television and cinema. Even the average household might one day be equipped with such a device: a small console linked to a central computerized memory or experience bank that could be connected to the consumer's electrode terminals for the price of a few cents in electricity. Then the tuned-in consumer would have only to dial the code number of the desired experience—whether it be a night in bed with his favorite actress (guaranteed to be successful) or a precarious climb up Mount Everest (also guaranteed to be successful). It doesn't take much imagination to see how the phrase "Live Better Electrically" could cease to be a mere advertising slogan.

It was this sort of arrangement that Daniel E. Noble, vice-chairman of the board of Motorola, Inc., had in mind when he coined the phrase "electronic nirvana." The same sort of "library of vicarious living experiences" that he visualized for the turn of the century has been imagined by Arthur C. Clarke. With a nod to ESB progress, at the end of his book *Profiles of the Future,* Clarke states that "artificial memories, if they could be composed, taped and then fed into the brain electronically . . . would be a form of vicarious experience far more vivid (because affecting all of the senses) than anything that could be produced by the massed resources of Hollywood. They would, indeed, be the ultimate form of entertainment—a fictitious experience more real than reality."

When that day comes, the "frontier" man seems to require will be only a few bursts of electricity away.

FIVE

LIBERATING
THE SPIRIT

TOWARD "ELECTRONIC YOGA"
WITH BFT

It is possible, however, that we may find a plea-sure wave. Using feedback we may be able to train people to produce the sort of brainwave ac-tivity that accompanies a drug high. If that should happen, I suspect the transistor will be out-lawed.

—Dr. Joseph Kamiya
of Langley-Porter Neuropsychiatric
Institute

Theta training may very well facilitate awareness, enhance memory and, in general, lead to a sensa-tional increase in the efficiency with which the mind works.

—Dr. Barbara Brown
Chief of Experiential Physiology,
Veterans Administration Hospital,
Sepulveda

There is this emergent sacramentalism with re-gard to the feedback processes that I am sensing here. . . . You are getting into cultic relation-ships. . . . There are emergent shamans in your group.

—Dr. Jean Houston
of the Foundation for Mind Research

The idea that man can assert mind over body has persisted for centuries. In some Eastern cultures it has been taken for granted. Not so in the West. There have been spiritualists and "healers" here to be sure, but their "miracles" have generally been viewed with skepticism and often scorn by scientists and educated laymen. Prayer, an expression of the will, has been credited with everything from the dissolution of deadly tumors to the restoration of sight to the "hopelessly" blind. The lack of credible documentation, however, has made it easy to brush these claims aside, relegating them to the refuse heap of wishful thinking and fanatical religiosity. Now, suddenly, there is substantive evidence that the mind *can* work miracles, that impalpable thought *can* control matter, even heal it of its ills.

The pervasive drug culture that dawned in the 1960s, perhaps more than anything else, was instrumental in popularizing the idea of "inner space," the concept of an internal human reality at least as important as the external man. With the aid of LSD, mescaline, marijuana and other "mind-expanding" or "mind-revealing" drugs, man, in considerable number, began to engage directly the consciousness, the mind, the inner self, treating as *real* the quantities declared by the dogma of behaviorism to be irrelevant (because unobservable and supposedly immeasurable) in computing the sums of psychology.

This, however, was only the beginning. While many abused the hallucinogenic drugs, others used them as stepping stones to attempt deeper, more controlled forays into the realm of inner space. While some pro-claimed that "acid" was the answer to everything—a short cut to nirvana—some of the more thoughtful "heads" wondered why so few Zen adepts were abdi-cating meditation for drugs. Could it be that they had something better? As guru stock skyrocketed, it ap-peared that something was conscious control over, rather than merely submission to, internal states of feeling and being.

Even some of the most skeptical members of be-haviorist-bombarded Western society began to sit up and take note when "establishment" science, unable to ignore the loud and frequent claims, entered the picture and declared that many dedicated Zen and yoga medi-tators were indeed as good as their word. Researchers wired them to electroencephalogram (EEG) machines and other monitoring devices and found that they could, by sheer force of will, beefed up by years of training, produce on command profound trance states, raise and lower their blood pressure, reduce body temperature, slow their heart rates and, in general, tap into physiological functions said for decades to be forever beyond the reach of conscious control.

Now, with the dawning of the bio-cybernetic seven-ties, it is not too surprising that LSD and the other hallucinogens of the sixties are about to be eclipsed, in a sense, by an electronic successor: BFT. Bio-feed-back Training, or "electronic yoga" as it has been called, puts you in touch with inner space just like LSD but, unlike acid, leaves you in full control of your senses. And, unlike meditation, it doesn't take years of sitting on mountaintops to master. It gives strong indication of being safe and predictable and promises to revolutionize psychology and medicine as nothing else ever has. Bio-feedback pioneers say that BFT could, among other things, completely replace many drugs, help people overcome anxieties, overwhelm numerous psychosomatic ills, facilitate learning, enhance memory, alleviate heart and circulatory diseases, illuminate the many processes of the mind and even provide access to previously unimagined experiences, thus not only defining the dimensions of inner man but also extending those dimensions in the process.

VINDICATION FOR THE MAHARISHI

Zazen, which in Japanese means "sitting in meditation," attracted some Western scientists as early as the 1950s, but it wasn't until the late 1960s that psychologists, physiologists and others began making a concerted effort to find out what was really happening during the meditative trance. The fact that Zen practitioners had been practicing the art of meditation since ancient times indicated that *something* must be happening. Among the first to use modern science in the study of meditation were, appropriately enough, Japanese scientists. A research team at Komazawa University in Tokyo, led by psychologist Dr. Yoshiharu Akishige and psychiatrist Dr. Akira Kasamatsu, applied electrocardiograms, electroencephalographs, computers and other monitoring devices to the task.

In one of their first studies in 1969 the Tokyo team worked with forty-eight Zen priests and nuns, along with a control group of one hundred subjects unschooled in meditation. Surprisingly the sitting position of *zazen* alone was found to effect some physiological changes, not only in the meditators but also in several of the controls. Once on the floor, stiff-backed and cross-legged, their respiratory rate diminished to a mere four or five breaths per second (as opposed to the normal seventeen or more); in several cases body temperature dropped a few degrees; and pulse fell ten to fifteen beats a minute below the normal in each case.

Dr. Akishige believes that these changes can be explained, in part, by the strain that the *zazen* position places on the diaphragm. This, he says, "affects the autonomous nervous system and the over-all result is a calming influence, a slowing down of the bodily functions."

As for brain activity during the deep trance state, the researchers found no correlation here with either sleep or hypnotic trance. The meditators, but not the controls, seemed suspended in a unique limbo region that was unlike normal wakefulness and normal sleep. What intrigued the Tokyo workers most was the fact that, unlike the controls, the Zen adepts were profoundly detached from external stimuli. The EEGs of controls who had assumed the *zazen* position revealed significant interruption in brain-wave pattern following auditory stimulation. The sounding of an electric bell threw squiggles into their EEGs that lasted fifteen seconds and longer. The Zen meditators, on the other hand, successfully "screened" out the distracting bell, showing, typically, only a two-second interruption in brain-wave pattern. They demonstrated similarly impressive detachment when challenged with numerous other forms of stimulation.

Dr. Kasamatsu, the team's research psychiatrist, noted at the conclusion of these experiments that Zen meditation may be of great value in the treatment of the mentally and emotionally disturbed. "It is important for a patient who has been mentally ill and who is about to return to society," he explained, "to have a sense of detachment. He realizes that he has been ill and perhaps still is. Practicing *zazen* may help him dispel his anxieties and achieve a feeling of detachment." As we shall see, BFT offers an even better way of achieving a state of detached tranquillity, a way of speeding up proficiency in something approaching the meditative art.

Other evidence that meditation opens the way to asserting mind over matter comes from an unlikely source: a study of the work of Maharishi Mahesh Yogi, the crafty, giggling guru who became almost as famous in the 1960s as many of his disciples (the Beatles, Mia Farrow, Shirley MacLaine and others). At first dismissed by science as nothing more than a colorful fraud, the Maharishi and his school of Transcendental Meditation (TM) are now accorded a growing respect by the scientific community.

TM, which, as it turns out, originated in India six thousand years ago, got its first medical examination in 1970, under the direction of Dr. Robert Keith Wallace, an experimental physiologist at the Center for the Health Sciences in Los Angeles. As his subjects, Dr. Wallace chose fifteen college students who were practicing TM, as taught by the Maharishi. Dr. Wallace himself was instructed by the Maharishi in the proper technique, which reputedly can be learned in four one-hour practice sessions, spread over four days. To get into the trance state, the subject positions himself in a chair, closes his eyes and chants a rhythmic "TM cue signal" called the "Mantrum." It's a seemingly meaningless "Ugh-Ugh-Om-Om" sound, but it provides something on which to focus the mind and shut out distracting external stimuli as one approaches the meditative state. Though it is, in some regards, similar to self-hypnotic technique, the meditative trance that results is wholly unlike the hypnotic state.

Dr. Wallace's subjects were between nineteen and twenty-five years of age; all were described as "normal, with no physical or mental disability." They had each practiced TM for at least six months at the time they were examined. Some had practiced it for three years. All were serious about it, practicing daily for fifteen to twenty minutes in both the morning and the evening, as prescribed by the Maharishi.

Dr. Wallace found that TM was capable of producing measurable and, in some cases, dramatic effects on important physiological functions. He found it capable of producing "a fourth state of consciousness" distinct from wakefulness, deep sleep and dreaming. "Perhaps in such meditation, the ancient Hindu Yogis discovered or stumbled upon a form of human hibernation, a milder form of the winter sleep of animals," Dr. Wallace declared.

He studied the effects of TM on eight bodily processes. He found that results varied from subject to subject but that in all cases the results confirmed the existence of a unique state of consciousness. He took readings before and after meditation and as each subject slipped into the trance state, and then again as each achieved deep trance. In this way he was able to make comparative observations.

In addition to the brain-wave findings, he observed that oxygen consumption was rapidly diminished by TM. It generally takes eight hours of good sleep to decrease oxygen consumption by 20 per cent; yet it took only ten to fifteen minutes to descend to this level while practicing TM. Heart rate diminished by five beats per minute, and the flow of blood decreased by 25 per cent. Other indices of tranquillity—diminished blood lactate and increased electrical resistance of the skin—also provided proof of TM's efficacy. On the average, the level of ionized lactic acid salt particles in the blood stream fell off by 50 per cent from pre-TM periods. This indicates greatly diminished stress since lactate levels are known to rise in direct proportion to anxiety. Tense, anxious feelings also tend to stimulate the sweat glands, decreasing electrical resistance of the skin, making it easier for electrical current to pass through it. Under TM, the subjects' resistance to electrical current *increased* a stunning 500 per cent.

Since TM is relatively easy to learn, Dr. Wallace suggests that it might be useful in quelling both physical and mental tensions. It may even come in handy in space travel, where it could combine a wakeful, alert state of mind with low-oxygen consumption. Indeed, the Stanford Research Institute announced plans in mid-1970 to follow through on Dr. Wallace's work and see whether TM could become a useful part of the astronauts' curriculum. Besides diminishing their consumption of oxygen without affecting their alertness, TM may also provide an answer to other problems of long-term space travel, such as irritability, tension, anxiety, boredom.

According to Dr. Herbert Benson of Harvard University School of Medicine, TM may have more down-to-earth applications as well. He reports that nineteen men, twenty-one to thirty-eight years of age, found TM preferable to the drugs they had used for some time. These included marijuana, barbiturates, LSD and heroin. After getting "hooked" on TM, all of them gave up the drugs which they then found, in Dr. Benson's words, "extremely distasteful."

GETTING HIGH ON ALPHA

Though TM certainly appears to be a more reliable key than LSD for unlocking the intricacies of the inner mind, it, too, leaves something to be desired. Its effects are general rather than specific and the "user" has no way of knowing for sure just how much progress he is making. Some further refinement is needed, a more finely tooled key, one capable of opening all of the doors of perception, with precision and delicacy. It appears now that BFT may be that key.

As stated above, there are those who believe that bio-feedback training may not only illuminate the myriad workings of the mind but may even fling open the doors to entirely new kinds of experience, extending the inner dimensions of the emergent cybernetic man. One of these is Dr. Joseph Kamiya, a research specialist with Langley-Porter Neuropsychiatric Institute in San Francisco and a lecturer in medical psychology at the University of California School of Medicine. "I may be an optimist," he says, "but I do believe that the next step in man's evolution will be in the experiential domain." As one of the foremost explorers of that domain, Dr. Kamiya set the stage as early as 1958 for the current explosion in BFT research.

Explaining that early work, Dr. Kamiya notes that the brain produces electrical activity that can be visualized—with the help of an EEG machine—in the form of constantly changing wave patterns. Electrical signals, picked up by electrodes attached to the scalp with a special conductive glue, are translated onto graph paper by the EEG machine, revealing brain waves of varying frequencies and amplitudes. Four primary brain-wave patterns have been identified using this technique—delta, theta, alpha and beta, all contained within a total energy spectrum of about zero to forty cycles per second.

Alpha, which moves at a frequency of eight to twelve cycles per second, happens to be the most prominent type of brain-wave activity, and, because it can be traced so easily by EEG, Dr. Kamiya seized upon it when he decided to see whether a subject could be taught *awareness* of an internal state, in this case one that nearly all of us slip in and out of from perhaps five to thirty times each minute, without, of course, ever knowing it.

Dr. Kamiya and his associates, then at the University of Chicago, wired a subject for EEG, placed him in a darkened room and then monitored his brain waves from an adjacent cubicle. The subject was instructed to close his eyes and guess whether he was in "state A" (alpha) or "state B" (non-alpha) whenever a bell rang. He was told after each guess whether he was right or wrong. Given this sort of feedback, the subject quickly learned to discriminate between the two states. He went from 50 per cent accuracy (no better than chance) on the first day to 100 per cent accuracy on the fourth day, making the correct guess 400 times in a row. Other subjects were tested with similar results. And once the subjects had learned to discriminate between the two states, it developed that they could switch either state on or off at will, on command from the experimenters!

Since moving to Langley-Porter, Dr. Kamiya has altered his experimental procedure somewhat and now trains subjects to sustain or repress alpha without first undergoing the discrimination exercise. Subjects are, typically, placed in darkened, soundproof rooms and told to attempt to sustain an audio-feedback tone (which goes on whenever the subject is in an alpha state) or, alternately, to try to keep it off. Dr. Kamiya considers 70 per cent success at this "convincing" and observed that most subjects achieve this after only four or five hours of training. Some subjects become so proficient that they can keep alpha "on" for days or switch it on and off at will, without any feedback whatever.

"All of this is very important to us," Dr. Kamiya says, "because it shows that man is capable of achieving and controlling various states of consciousness that he is normally only vaguely aware of, if at all, states ordinarily so elusive that he is unable to grasp them." Then, too, there are the therapeutic possibilities. When they try to explain how they learn to sustain alpha, subjects typically observe that they begin to associate with the sounding of the tone a feeling of serenity, detachment, drifting, but at the same time a feeling of alertness so that the state is unlike drowsiness. Some find it highly pleasurable and even begin to talk of getting an "alpha high." ("It used to be that I had to pay subjects to come in for experiments," Dr. Kamiya says. "Now I've got more volunteers than I know what to do with.") Most important, an almost complete lack of anxiety seems to accompany the alpha state, suggesting that it might become a useful electronic tranquilizer, liberating thousands from chemical sedatives, hypnotics and soporifics—and from the damaging and sometimes addicting side effects that accompany them.

But as for alpha becoming a substitute for euphoriant drugs or deep meditation of the Zen variety, Dr. Kamiya has his doubts. He concedes that some heavy alpha "users" express feelings of "being very, very much with it" during high alpha periods but says that most do not get this intense a reward out of it. "It is possible, however," he continues, "that we may find a pleasure wave. Using feedback, we may be able to train people to produce the sort of brain-wave activity that accompanies a drug high." But, he adds wryly, "if that should ever happen, I suspect the transistor will be outlawed."

Dr. Kamiya's work with practiced Zen meditators indicates that alpha is probably an important part of their art but not the whole picture. "I do think here again, however, that it will be possible to find the unique neurophysiological signature of meditation by checking out other channels—besides alpha. Once we have the complete physiological pattern that characterizes meditation there's no reason why we can't train people, with feedback, to mimic it in a relatively short period of time."

CEREBRAL LIGHT SHOWS

One of the leading BFT researchers looking into channels beyond alpha is Dr. Barbara Brown, chief of Experiential Physiology at Sepulveda Veterans Administration Hospital in Southern California. A psychopharmacologist and psychophysiologist with the development of five important drugs to her credit, Dr. Brown is one of the most enthusiastic proponents of BFT. Her laboratory houses what is probably the most sophisticated feedback complex in the country. Apart from alpha (which she has trained subjects to produce "in beautiful quantity" with the eyes *open*), Dr. Brown is working with beta and theta waves and with a number of other physiological functions.

Her subjects watch the "music" of their minds and bodies flicker across various screens in a dazzling but meaningful matrix of colors, each coded to a different function. There's feedback for alpha and gastric acidity (the latter picked up by tiny, painless monitors in the stomach), body temperature and beta, eye movements and theta, muscle activity, heart rate and pulse pressure. One literally confronts one's inner self—and learns how to manipulate it. Just as subjects quickly learn to control alpha, so do they become adept at exercising their wills over all of these other functions. It's not difficult to understand why Dr. Brown's cerebral light shows, starring the subject himself, have been attracting volunteers in record numbers. She now has a backlog of more than five hundred would-be subjects.

The research in theta and beta waves has begun to yield some enticing information. Theta, which Dr. Brown defines as "that rhythmic EEG activity of from four to seven cycles per second," seems to be related, she says, to problem solving, sorting and filing of incoming data and retrieval of information deposited in the brain's memory bank. Dr. Brown is heartened enough by her findings to declare that "theta training may very well facilitate awareness, enhance memory and, in general, lead to a sensational increase in the efficiency with which the mind works."

Beta falls into a fast-paced fourteen to twenty-eight cycles per second, beyond which the human mind rarely ventures, hitting its highest limits only rarely and for fractions of a second. Dr. Brown has found, among other things, that heavy smokers generate an unusually large amount of beta. And, unlike the non-smoker or light smoker, these individuals exhibit very little alpha. Dr. Brown finds "absolutely irresistible" an experiment she is about to launch, in which she will attempt to train some of these high-strung betas to become cool, serene alphas. Will they then stop smoking and settle down to enjoy things at a pace more conducive to longer life? According to Dr. Brown, "It seems entirely possible. Even likely."

ELECTRONIC MEDICINE

In addition to her laboratory work, Dr. Brown is now occupied with the chairmanship of the Bio-Feedback Research Society, which she helped found. The Society has enjoyed phenomenal growth and now has over three hundred members. At its first national conference, conducted in California in late 1969, 142 scientists were in attendance. From reports presented at that symposium, Dr. Brown has compiled a list of some of the most significant areas in which BFT may have profound impact. Several have already been suggested. Among others:

Athletics—"Perfection in athletic accomplishments is acquired largely through mental concentration to produce an optimally integrated physical sequence of events," Dr. Brown notes. "The individual can just as easily practice the mental state away from the practice area, using the feedback signals from his brain waves and muscle states to signal moments of optimal preparation."

Appetite control—"When the compulsion to eat exists," she says, "the physiology and brain waves reflect this 'drive' state. The individual can train himself to recognize such a state by means of signals of his physiologic activity—which are displayed to him. He can then train himself to distinguish between the states and continue to produce a non-compulsive state."

Preventive medicine and psychosomatic ills—"The physiologic activity of each troublesome system," Dr. Brown explains, "can be used to feed back information about its own functioning. These can be heart rate, blood pressure, respiration, skin temperature, gastric acidity, intestinal motility, muscles, etc."

Heart-rate control—"Here it appears that feedback techniques can be of use in at least two major areas: (1) a wide variety of cardiac irregularities, particularly tachycardia, bradycardia, extra systoles and auricular flutter, and (2) psychologic anxiety and fear reactions." Dr. Peter Lang, research professor of psychology at the University of Wisconsin, among others, has achieved considerable success in this area. His subjects learn "to drive their own hearts" with video feedback screens on which are projected lines corresponding to their heart rates. The shorter the line, the slower the heart rate, and the patients quickly learn to shorten them up.

Blood-pressure control—"This sort of control," says Dr. Brown, "may prove to be a life-saving procedure, providing the patient with the ability to maintain his blood pressure low enough to prevent development of both the symptoms of high blood pressure (headaches, dizziness) as well as preventing the more serious results of high blood pressure, such as coronary attacks, strokes and kidney damage." Among those most active in this field, building on the seminal animal experiments of Dr. Neal E. Miller of Rockefeller University, are Drs. David Shapiro and Bernard Tursky of Harvard Medical School (see "Visceral Learning" below).

Skin-temperature control—"A fairly easy physiologic activity which individuals can learn to bring under voluntary control is the temperature of the hand or even a single finger," Dr. Brown observes. "Many processes involve constriction of the blood vessels. With feedback training, this vasoconstriction can be markedly reduced, with the consequent relief from pain and coldness." Scientists getting good results here include Elmer and Alyce Green of the Menninger Foundation in Kansas. Using temperature feedback, several of their subjects have been relieved of chronic headaches of the migraine variety. The Greens also suggest that "starvation and absorption of tumors through blood flow control" appears possible.

Muscle control—"Individuals suffering from muscle tension due to anxiety or who suffer fatigue or general fatigue benefit from training to induce muscle relaxation," Dr. Brown explains, noting that Dr. John V. Basmajian of Emory University has trained several of his subjects to "fire" specific, *individual* muscle cells at will. Firing of the electrical energy within the cell is amplified to provide audio feedback, and some subjects become so skillful that they can actually fire off cells in rhythmic sequences so that it sounds as if they are playing the drums. Speaking before a scientific symposium in Iowa, Dr. Basmajian said, "There is no limit to the number of applications in research and technology that are possible from the basic knowledge that, given electronic feedback, man can consciously control individual motorneurons with exquisite precision." Among those applications are control of muscle spasms without drugs, induced relaxation and the manipulation of cellular activity to control prosthetic devices without many of the encumbering mechanisms that are required today.

Education—Here Dr. Brown notes that many have proposed teaming BFT with the upcoming crop of computer-assisted teaching machines. "It is well known," she says, "that the attention span of children is short. An accurate indicator of the length of each span of attention would be extremely useful in maximizing the use of teaching machines. Ideally, the display screen of the teaching machine would be capable of changing color: green, let us say, for periods when the child's attention level is high, constituting a go-ahead signal. And red for periods when attention begins to wander —a stop signal. The color of the screen would be controlled by two basic brain-wave patterns—one associated with high attention levels and the other associated with non-attention." Sophisticated successors to this first type of machine might tap into the brain-wave activities so that they could gauge the child's receptivity to specific types of information at specific times.

VISCERAL LEARNING

About the same time that Dr. Kamiya began his experiments with alpha, proving that individuals can learn awareness and control of internal mental states, Dr. Neal Miller of Rockefeller University was setting out to demonstrate that similar voluntary controls can be imposed on the internal organs, on the "viscera." Most, to put it mildly, thought Dr. Miller was going out on a limb. After all, it was well established that the internal organs are controlled by the autonomic nervous system, which, by definition, is supposed to be independent of the will and not susceptible to conscious control. Only those responses mediated by the cerebrospinal (voluntary) nervous system, involving skeletal movements, could be consciously manipulated—or so the textbooks insisted.

The only sort of conditioning that had been applied to the autonomic nervous system, up to the time that Dr. Miller began his experiments, was the classical Pavlovian variety. But Dr. Miller was convinced that visceral responses, just like skeletal responses, *could* be learned and controlled at will. Ten years ago he performed what appears, at first glance, to have been an extremely simple experiment. But, as it turned out, it was an experiment that would help overturn some of the most widely adhered-to theories of behavioral learning.

Dr. Miller's historic experiment involved two groups of dogs. One group was rewarded with water for increasing salivation, while the other was rewarded for decreasing salivation. The experiment proved that animals can change normal patterns of salivation, not in one direction only, but in any direction that produces rewards. Thus, at last, it was demonstrated that a response mediated by the autonomic nervous system *is* susceptible to non-classical conditioning. Pavlovian conditioning could only have excited an increase in salivation *or* a decrease—not both. And it had been believed up to this time that the bodily structures controlled by the autonomic system were susceptible only to this very crude, unidirectional conditioning.

Dr. Miller's experiment showed that this was not the case. He demonstrated that visceral responses can be mediated by *operant* conditioning or learning, in which rewards can be used to reinforce *any* behavior that immediately precedes the reward. Thus, too, it was demonstrated that the autonomic system was by no means as "stupid" and inflexible as had always been believed, that it was susceptible to sophisticated, consciously adaptable forms of conditioning.

Even then, however, Dr. Miller had his troubles. Science had been "down" on the autonomic system so long that it couldn't readily accept the new findings. It was rather like suddenly being told that an idiot child is really a genius after all. "For years," Dr. Miller remembers, "students and research assistants who were supposed to be working on the problem kept finding excuses to do something else instead. The prejudice against visceral learning was just too strong. The autonomic nervous system was just not held in high esteem, at least in this country. It's a cultural matter. Someone has said, for instance, that North Americans think with their skeletal muscles, while people in South America think with their glands."

Then, too, doubts remained in some minds about the interpretation of the results of that first experiment. Salivation is generally said to be a visceral response but some feared that the dogs might somehow have learned to regulate salivation via the voluntary system. To prove that this was not the case, Dr. Miller and his principal associate Dr. Leo DiCara devised a way of putting the cerebrospinal system completely out of the picture. Then, they reasoned, if the same response was obtained there could be no question about its origin. Using curare, the researchers paralyzed the skeletal muscles of rats, thus blocking transmission of cerebrospinal nerve impulses. The curare, however, had no effect on the autonomic system, letting internal organs continue to function normally. (Since the lungs rely upon skeletal muscle movement they were artificially respirated.)

Food and water could not be used as rewards under the circumstances, so Dr. Miller employed electronic stimulation of the brain, exciting the "pleasure centers" whenever he wanted to reinforce a certain visceral response. Mild shock was also used, simply to demonstrate that ESB is not the only thing that can reinforce visceral behavior. The reward, in this case, was *avoidance* of shock. Using this ingenious experimental design, Dr. Miller and his colleagues found that the curarized rats could be taught to raise and lower their heart rates (by as much as 20 per cent in either direction after only ninety minutes of training), to alter the rate of urine formation, change blood pressure, and decrease or increase blood flow through specific bodily structures.

The specificity of control that could be learned was particularly significant, since physiologists had long maintained that the autonomic system functions as a general unit. Dr. Miller found that this is not the case, that the system can be trained to exhibit specificity, in which one visceral function can be altered without affecting the others in any way. The sophistication that the system is capable of in this regard was dramatically demonstrated when the research team trained rats to dilate the blood vessels in one ear only—a sophistication even Dr. Miller calls "eerie."

Dr. Brown has suggested several of the disorders that might be corrected by visceral learning effected through feedback training systems. And a number of medical centers are now at work training human subjects to control heart rate and blood pressure; these centers include Harvard University Medical School, Cornell University Medical College and the Gerontology Research Center in Baltimore. Results are encouraging. At Cornell, for example, one victim of five heart attacks has been trained to reduce his heart rate from a dangerous 100 beats a minute to fewer than 70. Elderly heart patients at the Gerontology Center in Baltimore have achieved similar results with feedback training. New York City's Bellevue Hospital has initiated a large project designed to train vulnerable people to lower their blood pressure. Once trained, individuals can control their heart rates and blood pressure without further feedback training for protracted periods. Some have gone sixteen months without "refresher courses."

Typical of the visceral-learning centers is the one at Harvard, under the direction of psychologist David Shapiro and psychophysiologist Bernard Tursky. Among the first to begin work with human patients, they have a complex, computerized laboratory in which subjects are trained to control visceral responses with the help of audio-visual feedback. The subject is placed in a soundproof room where he is attached to numerous monitoring devices—electrodes, blood pressure cuffs and so on. He sits in a comfortable chair facing a screen and is told only that the researchers are interested in the degree to which subjects can learn to control responses that are said to be involuntary. The subject, in this case, is not told which responses he will be conditioned to make—since the major concern at this point is still with the experimental rather than the therapeutic. By keeping the subject in the dark about the response that will be sought, there is no risk of his actively trying to achieve the desired results. To further insure against any extraneous influence on the outcome, the researcher flips a coin twice to decide which of four possible responses will be conditioned.

The subject is told only that when he makes the desired response (by chance to begin with) a white light will go on the screen and a beep will be heard.

It is his job to keep the light on and sustain the beep as much as possible. These are his rewards for making the "right" visceral responses. In addition, he is told that as an extra reward a picture will be displayed across a larger screen after every twelve lights and beeps. Then the researchers leave the room, the lights dim and the experiment is on.

Suppose the response that is sought is a *simultaneous* lowering of both blood pressure and heart rate. Even though the subject doesn't know that this is the response that he is supposed to try for, it is a response that is bound to occur randomly, though perhaps only very fleetingly, at various points in time. When it *does* occur, the light goes on and the beep sounds. Gradually, simply because the subject wants that reward, he learns to call back the light and beep with increasing frequency and control. At first it's just a matter of hoping that it will come back; later he may make subjective judgments about the "feeling state" that successfully elicits the desired state. Most subjects make progress in their first sessions, many learning to lower their heart rates ten beats per minute or more.

HYPNOTIC CONTROL

Though hypnotherapy does not rely upon bio-feedback training, it appears to provide another approach to visceral learning. Recent hypnosis research provides further evidence that man is capable of controlling the "uncontrollable." Dr. Philip G. Zimbardo, codirector of the Stanford University Hypnosis Research Center, has reported that he and his colleagues have trained subjects to vary temperatures simultaneously in their right and left hands by as much as seven degrees. Subjects were placed in a room carefully maintained at a constant 83° F. Under hypnosis, the subjects were told to concentrate on their hands, making one hotter and the other colder. Just why they were able to do this, why hypnosis gave them the means to control a part of the involuntary system, is not yet fully understood, though one persuasive theory is discussed later in this chapter.

Though the effects of hypnosis are by no means yet as predictable (nor perhaps as safe) as those of BFT, some that have been reported are truly astonishing. One Portland dentist, Dr. Irl Clary, for example, reports that he is using hypnosis to reduce pain and swelling and even to stop bleeding. "It is hard to believe until you have seen it," he told those assembled at the 1969 meeting of the Society for Clinical and Experimental Hypnosis. Dr. Howard B. Miller, delivering a paper at the same conference, enlarged on the seemingly miraculous effects of hypnotherapy, reporting that it may be useful even in the treatment of cancer.

Dr. Miller reports that some striking results with cancer patients have led him to believe "that the involuntary nervous system is not as involuntary as previously thought, that it may be a major factor in many disease conditions, as well as in the pathological changes that occur during the course of disease. In fact, the cases studied strongly suggest that the involuntary nervous system is not involuntary at all. The cases observed tend to show it is more under our conscious control than previously believed." Consequently, Dr. Miller states, it is probably a serious mistake to separate diseases into "organic" and "functional" categories, adding that the involuntary system should be used in the treatment of all types of disease. The extraordinary results that can be obtained by its utilization in treatment are dramatized in the following case histories, excerpted from Dr. Miller's paper "Emotions and Malignancy":

Two women, one with asthma, and one with duodenal ulcer, were being given suggestions to encourage and enhance their ability for emotional and physical relaxation. Both women had associated breast tumors. The asthma patient had a malignant tumor, determined by needle biopsy; the duodenal ulcer patient had a tumor which was benign. Both women had refused surgery previously. While under treatment for their respective problems of asthma and duodenal ulcer, the associated breast tumors in both patients resolved significantly. The benign tumor disappeared completely, while the malignant one shrank to less than one-fourth its original size. Suggestions were being given for calmness and relaxation, increased feeling of confidence, security and, in addition, for an increase in healing power and rapid tissue repair with normal cell replacement and function. A determined effort was also made to guide the person away from her presenting fear to herself. Treatments were continued for twice a month for four to six months, then once a month to date. It is now one-and-a-half years later that they have been observed. The situation remains at that level.

Motivated by this experience, two cases of carcinoma of the cervix were accepted in treatment. Both had refused surgery previously. The suggestions were the same as in the breast cases. Both cases resolved significantly. One went from a cytological classification of Class IV (malignant) to a dyskaryosis (which is a border-line type). The other case regressed to a hyperactive, but negative class. Both have remained in this state for one year.

Dr. Miller reports on another case, a man with lupus erythamatosus, a serious skin eruption with accompanying blood problem. The condition can be fatal. The man was undergoing hypnotherapy, however, for another reason. He was suffering from colitis and hoped that the hypnosis would help him achieve the degree of serenity needed to avoid further aggravation of that disorder. Unexpectedly, in the course of hypnotherapy, the blood and skin problems disappeared. Another LE victim was then purposely sought out and given the same hypnotherapy for general relaxation. The LE again rapidly disappeared.

Because of these encouraging results, the effects of hypnosis on the levels of other blood elements were investigated. "A marked reduction to normal limits,"

Dr. Miller says, "was possible in cases of elevated cholesterol, steroids, blood sugar and catacholamines." It was also possible to *raise* the levels of these blood elements. The altered chemical level, achieved in each case without dietary change, could then be maintained with posthypnotic suggestion. Bleeding, as suggested by Dr. Clary, is also susceptible to hypnotic suggestion. Dr. Miller notes that abnormal bleeding following tooth extraction has been abated in two cases "with no abnormal bleeding, in either case, with further dentistry." Uterine bleeding that resisted all other forms of treatment has also been checked with hypnosis.

How can hypnosis have such far-reaching effects? Dr. Miller has proposed a theory which, while it does not detail the specific mechanics of hypnosis, does provide a compelling explanation of its general cause and effect. He observes that even though the pituitary and hypothalamus have generally been considered to be the control centers of the involuntary system, the *true* center may in fact be the cerebral cortex, in which higher thought processes originate. The reason for this contention is the fact that the cerebral cortex secretes numerous neurocirculatory hormones that have strong effects on the pituitary and hypothalamus—perhaps much stronger than anyone suspected. If we accept the idea that it is the cerebral cortex that is in control of the hormonal and nervous systems, then it is not difficult to appreciate the far-reaching effects emotional stress (mediated in the cortex) can have on the body, right down to each of its individual cells. In the hormone system, the deleterious effect proceeds, in the Miller hypothesis, from the cerebral cortex to the hypothalamus to the pituitary to the adrenal to the cells. In the nervous system the effect moves from the cerebral cortex to the sympathetic (and along a separate channel to the parasympathetic) nervous system to the cells.

Dr. Miller notes that thought, generated in the cerebral cortex, is really a form of energy—a stimulus that can send an electrical current down any nerve to the affected tissue. Excess stimulation channeled through either the hormonal or nervous systems, he says, "will lead to bio-chemical and structural disorganization and final dissolution if a sufficient rest period is not allowed for recovery. Anxiety, acute or chronic, is therefore as potent a disrupter of cellular organization as any foreign substance." Hypnosis, he says, acts to *block* the transmission of anxiety by altering thought processes within the cerebral cortex.

THE WAVE OF THE FUTURE

Perhaps because they have enjoyed so much success in so short a period of time, scientists exploring the experiential domain and particularly those involved in BFT research are now predicting things that would certainly have been regarded as preposterous a few years ago. Dr. Brown, for example, foresees the complete collapse of mental hospitals when "brain-wave analyses of every individual will be made routinely. When an analysis reveals an incipient neurosis or psychosis, an individualized program for feedback can be supplied. The potential patient can then visit his neighborhood computer self-treatment center where he inserts the taped treatment program into the computerized feedback system and continues treatment until all signs of the potentially abnormal condition have disappeared." Others have suggested that feedback systems will be devised that will enable women to control their ovulation, providing the ultimate birth-control technique. Some even envision—for the more remote future—conscious control over cell death, so that aging can be slowed or even halted.

BFT may also provide some scientific means of investigating extrasensory perception (ESP). "Feedback," Dr. Brown says, "may be the great white hope for ESP," making it possible for researchers to identify the "neurophysiological signature" of the ESP state, if, in fact, such a state really exists. A BFT investigation of ESP is under way, and though no conclusions can yet be stated, there *is* evidence that those who score high on ESP tests do exhibit certain specific brain-wave patterns. For one thing, those who get the highest ESP scores also seem to generate significant amounts of alpha. No one is suggesting that these individuals are transmitting "thought" at alpha frequencies (the amount of energy involved is so minute that this would seem to be out of the question) but the finding does provide some sort of starting point—some place to begin sorting out the pieces. And it comes along in the nick of time, since many ESP researchers were despairing of ever finding any tool with which to get at this perplexing phenomenon.

Even if it is never possible to get people's thoughts perfectly aligned (so that, perhaps, thought transmission *could* occur), brain-wave research at least provides a means of categorizing the sort of cerebral rhythms that seem to characterize different types of people. And this is a capability that Dr. Grey Walter, the distinguished neurophysiologist, suggests be put to rather utopian use. World leaders, he notes, often have difficulty communicating with one another and this can create considerable risks for the rest of the population. The reason for these communicative barriers, he says, is the fact that many of these leaders have different types of brain rhythm.

Writing in one of the scientific journals of the United Nations, Dr. Walter states that it is possible to separate the world population into three distinct groups—non-visualists, pure visualists and mixed visualists, each of which has a distinctive brain-wave pattern. Should a visualist and a non-visualist (abstract thinker) get together, Dr. Walter asserts, they may have serious difficulty in agreeing on things, since they will be approaching the problem at hand "eye to ear" rather than eye to eye. Such problems, he says, may account for many of the irrational ruptures that occur among artists, scientists, politicians, administrators, diplomats and even married couples. In many cases, he adds, brain-wave incompatibility can destroy *all* chance for effective dialogue.

In the realm of diplomacy, Dr. Walter observes that

"the two antagonists think they are speaking the same language, but are not. Their mental accents, so to say, separate them as surely as verbal accents in a class-conscious society. . . . It may even be that serious crises between nations, where no territorial or material advantage can be gained by either side, have arisen because the negotiators have different types of imagery and can only talk at cross-purposes."

Dr. Walter, director of the Physiology Department of the Burden Neurological Institute and a professor at the University of Aix-Marseille in France, thinks the problems are of sufficient magnitude to warrant "brain-wave typing," at least for diplomats. Some world crises might be avoided, he says, if negotiators had their brain-rhythm types stamped inside their passports, as a matter of law. Thus it would be possible to avoid putting individuals who are *inherently* incompatible together at the negotiating table!

Ever more exciting, for the future, is the possibility that "creativity" might—for the price of a few cents in electricity—ultimately become a purchasable commodity. The Greens of the Menninger Foundation envision the possibility of enhancing creativity by training in the alpha-theta border region. "It is interesting to note," they observe in a scientific paper co-authored with E. Dale Walters, "that the psychological state associated with hypnagogic-like imagery has been reported by many outstanding thinkers as the condition in which their most valuable ideas come to them. To describe this state, they have used such phrases as the 'fringe of consciousness,' the 'off-consciousness,' the 'transliminal mind,' and 'reverie.' It is not difficult to imagine a research program in creativity in which brain-wave feedback is used for voluntary induction of that psychophysiological state, in the alpha-theta border region, which is associated with such descriptive statements." Though theta is normally associated with sleep or deep trance, the Greens have already trained individuals to exert such control over their internal states that some can communicate verbally while in the theta condition; some describe the state as "wakeful dreaming." Others seem to hallucinate vividly in the state.

Dr. Kamiya foresees yet another future capability accruing from brain-wave research: the ability to resist advertising, propaganda and behavioral manipulation. "People with full control of their internal states," he says, "might be better prepared to resist external control." Training for this purpose, he suggests, should be incorporated into the educational system: "Trained control of bodily states might well be added to the curriculum, perhaps beginning as early as elementary school." Dr. Kamiya concedes that both Madison Avenue and Washington, D.C., can be counted on to resist the idea, though once the brain-wave patterns associated with this sort of "resistance" are identified there will be nothing to prevent individuals, who have access to the proper equipment, from schooling themselves in hard-nosed skepticism.

INSTRUMENTING THE REVOLUTION

To hurry the day when the common man can reap some of the benefits of BFT, researchers are actively working to create inexpensive, portable bio-feedback trainers. Dr. Kamiya says that a number of large companies are developing such machines and predicts that they will be available within a year or two at a cost of less than two hundred dollars each. These will be capable of feeding back a wide spectrum of information from the body and the mind.

Dr. Brown is developing one of the most exotic pieces of feedback hardware—a device that translates brain and body signals into acceptable musical harmonics. With additional design, she adds, the instrument can also translate signals into visual art forms. She envisions mass production of the portable device at reasonable cost. With your own light-and-sound show, she says, you can learn to recognize "your own kind of music" and then detect, in plenty of time to do something about it, when you are "getting out of tune with yourself." Dr. Kamiya has proposed a similar device, but one that would utilize ordinary television sets for feedback display. And the Greens have already played what they call "the music of the hemispheres" or "biological music": brain-wave signals filtered through some of their non-portable auditory feedback systems.

Dr. Miller envisions the day when feedback systems the size of hearing aids will help people practice visceral control. Such devices may be only five years away, warning patients when their heart rates or blood pressures are beginning to rise, helping others ward off muscle spasms, epileptic seizures and so on.

Meanwhile, Dr. Wendell R. Lipscomb, chief of research in the Department of Mental Hygiene, Mendocino State Hospital, has developed an "encephalophone" that feeds back brain-wave information and might ultimately be used for such diverse purposes as detecting brain tumors and listening in on what a suspected criminal is thinking. With training, Dr. Lipscomb believes that brain-damaged patients can learn how to shift brain activity from an injured area to a counterpart area on the opposite side of the brain. Dr. Lipscomb and his colleagues use EEG signals to produce an audio-stereophonic effect, a form of music, really, that can be used to evaluate emotional health. Brain-wave signals picked up via electrodes attached to various parts of the scalp are amplified and played back over loudspeakers arranged in such a way that they correspond spatially to the geometry of the skull, that is, to the points on the skull from which they originate. Thus the subject is able not only to learn how to control general brain-wave patterns but also to exert control over the activity of specific brain areas.

Contemplating the possibilities, Dr. Lipscomb and his colleague John G. Sinclair, Jr., note that "with the development of a two-dimensional encephalophone we might find that control of the separate constituent waves of EEG is possible. We might be able to train subjects to move brain activity from one area to another, for example, from one hemisphere to another or even within one hemisphere. Such techniques may prove useful in brain retraining following surgery or injury. Perhaps the method may also provide new insight into the general process of learning and motivation. If one were to discover, for example, certain brain patterns that precede or accompany successful learning, one might be able to teach a process of mental preparation for learning that would involve voluntary control of brain patterns."

While the more complex devices are being readied by prestigious companies and large, well-funded research centers, the young are proceeding to make their *own* feedback machines (just as they learned how to synthesize their own hallucinogens in the sixties). Aquarius Electronics of Mendocino, California, run by a turned-on young entrepreneur, is already manufacturing a product called the "Aquarian Alphaphone." The AA is a relatively simple, battery-powered package that provides audio feedback for conditioning in the alpha state. With it, just about anyone can learn how to sustain an alpha high for hours on end.

What sort of controls will be imposed over the manufacture, sale and distribution of feedback devices remains to be seen. There is a fear among some that everything is moving too fast in this field, that the cultists and the faddists may "take over," as they did with LSD, giving the research effort a bad name, inviting uninformed government control. Indeed, one participant at the first national meeting of the Bio-Feedback Research Society in 1969, Dr. Jean Houston of the Foundation for Mind Research, observed that before long everyone will be saying, "Oh boy, you can program yourself against anxiety, to euphoria, to love, to whatever it is that you ought to. This is what, in cultures, has traditionally been performed by sacramental functions. And there is this emergent sacramentalism with regard to the feedback processes that I am sensing here. . . . You are getting into cultic relationships. . . . There are emergent shamans in your group."

While some counsel extreme caution, call for Food and Drug Administration control and so on, others point out that it is futile to worry at length about the cultists. One participant at the Bio-Feedback meeting pointed out that you can no more stop people from tinkering with feedback than you can stop them from smoking pot or drinking alcohol. Dr. Kamiya noted at that time that feedback systems are relatively easy to construct, and imaginative amateurs are bound to come up with models of their own. (And as we have just seen, this has already happened.) The best thing that the society can do, several agreed, is to prepare detailed guidelines for the proper use of feedback devices, pointing out some of the obvious dangers inherent in indiscriminately manipulating such things as heart rate and blood pressure.

"This is too important to let isolated cases of abuse stand in the way of research progress," Dr. Brown declares. "We mustn't let hysteria stand in the way, as it did with LSD, which could have become one of the most important research tools ever to come along." Dr. Brown is frankly opposed to FDA interference in bio-feedback research. "I don't really think we should have to proceed as we do with a new drug—to determine safety, efficiency—because the effects of feedback are predictable. We've got a tremendous amount of historical data in the Zen and yoga material. Furthermore, society needs this now. We've got this monstrous limbo area in which people are half sick, where they can't get any help, except at great expense and often through long years of therapy, the area of psychosomatic distress. And it is in this very area that feedback can do so much, where tension and anxiety can be alleviated with such ease."

She agrees wholeheartedly with the Greens, who conclude that "the most significant thing that may be facilitated through training in the voluntary control of internal states is the establishment of a Tranquillity Base, not in outer space but in inner space, on, or within, the lunar being of man."

INDEX

INDEX